W9-DAS-926

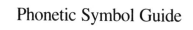

Phonetic Symbol Guide

Phonetic Symbol Guide

Geoffrey K. Pullum and
William A. Ladusaw

THE UNIVERSITY OF CHICAGO PRESS

Chicago and London

Geoffrey K. Pullum and William A. Ladusaw are both
on the linguistics faculty at the University of California,
Santa Cruz.

The University of Chicago Press, Chicago 60637
The University of Chicago Press, Ltd., London

95 94 93 92 91 90 89 88 87 86   54321

Library of Congress Cataloging-in-Publication Data

Pullum, Geoffrey K.
  Phonetic symbol guide.

  Bibliography: p.
  1. Phonetics—Notation.   I. Ladusaw, William A.,
1952–   .   II. Title.
P221.P85 1986   414   86-7036
ISBN 0-226-68531-4
ISBN 0-226-68532-2 (pbk.)

CONTENTS

TABLE OF ENTRIES

Diacritic Entries

ACKNOWLEDGMENTS

We would like to thank the many people who gave us encouragement and assistance during the preparation of this book.

For practical help, we thank Kenneth Christopher and Brigitte Ohlig, who assisted us with research and text-handling chores, and Daniel Wenger, whose technical know-how enabled us to access the Apple Laserwriter printer from both Macintosh and mainframe, making possible what would otherwise have been a thoroughly intractable job of manuscript preparation.

We greatly value the assistance of Aditi Lahiri and William Shipley (University of California, Santa Cruz), Peter Ladefoged and Ian Maddieson (UCLA), and, most of all, Karen Landahl (University of Chicago), who read right through various versions of the manuscript and gave us many helpful suggestions. With a generosity that touched us, these and other phoneticians and phonologists we consulted chose to welcome us as shipmates rather than repel us as boarders when we asked for the benefit of their specialized knowledge. We thought about all of their suggestions carefully, even though we decided not to implement some of them.

We also benefited from helpful conversations with Judith Aissen, Jane Collins, Nora C. England, Mary Haas, Jorge Hankamer, L. K. Richardson, and others, and we profited greatly from the detailed comments of several referees, who deserve better than to have their valuable contributions hidden from view by the cloak of anonymity accorded to publishers' consultants. We thank them for their close criticism and sensible suggestions, and absolve them, like the others who have assisted us, of blame for any errors that we have persisted in despite their best efforts.

INTRODUCTION

This book is primarily intended for use in the way that a dictionary is used. It provides a source in which the user can look up an unfamiliar phonetic or phonological symbol by reference to its form (its shape and graphic relationship to other symbols), and find an entry giving comprehensive guidance concerning its meaning (its recognized interpretation according to various traditions of scholarship in phonetics and phonology).

To some extent, the book can also be used as a guide to how to use phonetic symbols, and we have included a number of charts and other aids to the working linguist or phonetician with this in mind. Nevertheless we have a principally descriptive aim, not a prescriptive one: we explain how the symbols are employed in the literature of phonetics and linguistics, and we do not, for the most part, approve or proscribe specific usages. Likewise, the book is not intended as an introduction to phonetics; we presuppose, rather than supply, a grounding in phonetic theory (though we do supply a glossary of articulatory phonetic terminology which we hope will be useful).

Those who will most immediately and obviously benefit from this book include phoneticians, linguists, anthropologists, speech pathologists, audiologists, language teachers, translators, interpreters, speech engineers, philologists, and students of any of these subjects. But we hope that it will also be of use to those with a more peripheral interest in language who may encounter phonetic transcriptions in material they read.

What we have tried to do in this book, in short, is to collate and systematize information about the definitions for phonetic symbols that have been set down by recognized phonetic authorities, and about the actual usage that will be encountered in linguistic writings of all sorts.

We are general linguists, not primarily researchers in phonetics. However, between us we have taught phonetics and phonology in courses at various levels on a dozen campuses in Britain and the United States, and we have over thirty years of day-to-day acquaintance with the literature of the linguistic sciences. Moreover, we know what it is like to confront traditions conflicting with the ones in which we were trained: one of us was trained in the tradition associated with the International Phonetic Association (IPA) and later learned American transcription practices on the streets, and the other had the converse experience. In addition, we share an interest in typography and related matters that makes us sensitive to some of the minutiae that become relevant when one pays close attention to the interpretation of published phonetic transcriptions.

We believe that it has been an advantage to us to be working as experienced consumers of phonetic practice rather than primary purveyors of it. We are accustomed to reading work in the field of syntax and semantics where linguists with little interest in phonetics or phonology (or else their editors, publishers, and printers) have made errors regarding transcription that clearly indicate the need for a reference work such as the present one. Where a research specialist in phonetics might see no ambiguity in a given usage because detailed knowledge of the subject matter permitted instant disambiguation, we see the ambiguity and the danger of misinterpretation. We have plenty of first-hand experience of encountering materials in phonetic or phonological transcriptions that initially seem obscure or baffling, and this has guided us in deciding what needs clear explanation in a book like this.

In addition, we have no axes to grind: there may be phoneticians with strong opinions about whether '[y]' is properly used for a palatal glide or for a front rounded vowel, but not us. The view of phonetic transcriptional practice presented in this book is not tacitly subordinated to the viewpoint of any school of thought, because we belong to none. We have no aim beyond that of not being unnecessarily puzzled, hindered, or misled by the transcriptional practices we find in the literature that we consult.

THE SCOPE OF THIS BOOK

In making decisions about the content and format of the book it has been necessary to make many difficult decisions about what to include and exclude. We have not attempted to gather together in one volume every symbol ever used to represent a sound in the long history of phonetics and phonology, or, worse, every font variant or transform of all the symbols that have been used since the invention of printing. Our goal is to provide a background of general knowledge for the symbols that linguists, phoneticians, and other students of language are likely to encounter in reading either contemporary books and journals or older works that are important enough to be consulted today.

Transliteration and romanization are activities which are logically distinct from phonetic transcription, but in practice the distinction is sometimes very hard to draw. For example, only a thin line separates the International Phonetic Association's phonetic alphabet from the International African Institute's proposed African orthography, and only minor additional steps need be taken to arrive at such systems as the conventional transliteration of Russian into roman letters or the pinyin romanization for Chinese. Note also that Kenneth Pike's famous *Phonemics* (1947) was subtitled *A Technique for Reducing Languages to Writing*. We have therefore included here some comments about the common use of some symbols in orthographies and romanizations. Such comments are not intended to be comprehensive. Where they have been included, it is either because such uses of the symbol conflict with their phonetic interpretations and a possible misinterpretation of the romanization might result, or because the orthographic use supplied an interpretation which was taken over in the use of the character as a phonetic symbol (e.g. the Old English orthographic characters *Ash* and *Eth*).

Phonetic transcription practices are often inculcated through a complex history of practical experience rather than through a rigorously codified rulebook. Many people will not be able to say exactly where they picked up a given idea—say, that an umlaut over a vowel symbol indicates a reversal of backness, or that a dot under a consonant indicates a retroflex articulation—but will nonetheless feel that the convention is generally recognized and could be used productively to create new transcriptions where necessary. Moreover, the tacit understandings about transcription that govern some traditions— particularly the American tradition—represent not a firm common ground but one that shifts over time like any other cultural system. We have tried in this book to present explicitly two very clear traditions: that of the IPA, which is the clearest, having a recognized international governing body to sanction its recommendations, and a more tenuous tradition we identify as "American" (we discuss these two traditions further below).

Even the IPA position on many topics has shifted during the hundred years of the Association's existence, and in the case of our effort to interpret and codify an American tradition, we are to some extent creating a consensus through judicious selection among variants rather than reporting a consensus that already exists. Much the same is true for our references to other traditions such as that of Slavicists, Indologists, etc. In other words, the reader who expects all phonetic practice to be amenable to rigorous pigeonholing according to the categories mentioned in this book will be somewhat alarmed by the diversity that is actually found.

SCOPE OF THE REFERENCES

Part of what this book aims to do is to permit the user to develop a historical and comparative perspective on the business of phonetic transcription. Such a perspective is often not provided by a linguistics graduate education. In the interest of the rapid acquisition of a fixed set of transcriptional practices that will be regarded *pro tem* as correct for purposes of the class, a study of the variability found in the literature is (quite rightly) postponed. But the professional linguist or phonetician will find it desirable or even necessary to develop a considerable tacit understanding of the variability of transcription practices in order to become fully comfortable with the whole literature of linguistics through the years. We attempt here to provide some of the basis for such an understanding, and to leave enough of a bibliographical trail through the references we cite to permit the serious researcher to achieve much more than that.

We have not been (nor could we have been) exhaustive in the literature we cite in our references. But we have, we believe, referenced most of the works of major influence in the two traditions that we seek to document. Where we articulate a usage which we believe to be generally true of another group (historical linguists, Indologists, Slavicists, or whatever), we have cited a randomly chosen work in the area. The choice of these works has often been serendipitous or even just arbitrary, so we warn the reader not to consider us to be claiming that all such works are of equal influence in the linguistic community.

In our research for this book we have encountered a number of works which make recommendations regarding transcription systems which we have not included in the texts of our entries. These range from invented alphabets of gentleman scholars and dilettantes to serious works by linguists, missionaries, and anthropologists who were influential but did not ultimately become contributors to the two main traditions documented here. (For interesting surveys of some of these, see Albright 1958, Pitman and St. John 1969, and the edition of Lepsius 1863 by J. Alan Kemp, which contains much interesting auxiliary material and a large bibliography.) Among the systems we have had to exclude are some of the well thought-out and elegantly designed sets of symbols in the IPA tradition developed for the click sounds of various Khoisan languages. The novel symbols proposed by Doke (1926a, 144), for example, are not covered in this book, not having attained currency anywhere.

We have also encountered proposals that might become standard but are recent enough that their currency is not yet established. Among these, we should mention the proposals of Grunwell et al. (1960) for transcribing disordered speech and those of Bush et al. (1973, see Ingram 1976, 93). Many of these proposals are similar to standard IPA proposals or are rather crude iconic extensions of them. As they are not encountered in general linguistic and phonetic works, we have decided not to include them in our purview.

THE IPA TRADITION

The official names announced for the IPA at its foundation in 1886, namely *Association Phonétique International, Weltlautschriftverein,* and *International Phonetic Association,* make one thing quite clear: the IPA was internationalist from the outset. Although the original shared interest of the members was the application of phonetics to the teaching of languages, particularly English, a more general focus of interest emerged fairly rapidly. As early as 1886, Otto Jespersen suggested that a phonetic alphabet applicable to all languages be devised, and a first version was ready by 1888.

The principles that guided the construction of this alphabet are set out in the classic booklet *Principles of the International Phonetic Association,* published by the IPA at University College London in 1949 and hereafter cited as *Principles.* These principles are mostly the same ones that guide the council of the IPA in making its decisions down to the present. (One exception is that an early effort to make IPA symbols as similar as possible to their correspondents in ordinary orthographies has been abandoned, clarity and distinctness being considered more important.) They are five in number. We paraphrase them here; for the original formulation, see *Principles*, pp. 1–2.

1. Wherever possible, differently shaped letters (not just diacritically modified letters) should be used for any two sounds that can distinguish one word from another in a single language.

2. Wherever possible, a single letter should be used for two sounds that are so similar that they never distinguish one word from another in a single language.

3. Wherever possible, only letter shapes that harmonize typographically with the letters of the roman alphabet should be used.

4. Wherever possible, use diacritics only in four circumstances: (i) for suprasegmental phenomena like length, stress, and intonation; (ii) for marking allophonic distinctions; (iii) where one diacritic can make it unnecessary to design a whole set of related new characters (e.g., with the tilde diacritic to indicate nasalized vowels); (iv) to represent minute shades of sound for scientific purposes.

5. Wherever possible, development of the alphabet should be along lines that accord with the phonemic principle and the Cardinal Vowel system.

It is an explicit attempt to follow these rules of thumb through the past century that has given rise to the IPA's current phonetic alphabet as surveyed in this book in the sections headed **IPA Usage**. The principles demand that there be as many distinct symbols as necessary, that there be no more distinct symbols than are necessary, that typographical appearance of symbols be taken seriously, that diacritical marks be kept to a minimum, and that phonetic transcription be grounded in scientific phonetics and phonology. They are sensible and carefully chosen. But as we shall see in the next section, these are not the only possible principles that could guide the development of a system of phonetic transcription.

THE AMERICAN TRADITION

The comments listed under the **American Usage** sections of the entries and some of the charts at the back are meant to document a tradition of transcription which has paralleled the development of the IPA but remained distinct from it on some points. Among the more obvious points of difference are the almost universal use among American linguists of the transcription '[ü]' for a high front rounded vowel in place of the IPA's '[y]' and the use of the wedge diacritic on symbols for palato-alveolar fricatives and affricates. It would be incorrect to suggest that American linguists do not know or use the IPA, but some conventions such as the ones just mentioned are almost universally used by American scholars, and quite generally supplant IPA recommendations. Because of their vitality and also their essential coherence, we believe it is proper to document them as a distinct tradition.

To accomplish this, it was necessary to induce from current and past practice an analog of the IPA's *Principles* manual for the American community. We began by considering the recommendations which have been published over the past 80 years of American linguistics and then sifted through them to find the ones which have caught on. These we have considered to be the basis of American usage, and they are sufficient to indicate points of possible confusion.

The American tradition has its roots in the practices of Americanists—the transcription practices arising from work beginning in the late 19th century on the indigenous languages of North America. After the publication of *The Handbook of American Indian Languages* (Boas ed. 1910), a committee of the American Anthropological Association consisting of Franz Boas, P. E. Goddard, Edward Sapir and A. L. Kroeber published recommendations for a transcription system to be used in the publication of texts and grammars of American languages (Boas et al. 1916).

These recommendations present a transcription system responsive to principles quite different from those of the IPA. While the IPA sought an alphabet which would provide symbols for "many minute shades of sound," offering "two distinct letters without diacritical marks" for sounds which contrasted in languages (*Principles,* p. 1), the Americanists sought a "practical" system for publication. It is practical in a number of respects. It explicitly seeks to avoid the creation of special characters which would not be available in standard faces and fonts, in order to expedite the publication of the texts. It sanctions a phonological approach to transcription, consigning phonetic detail to textual discussion in favor of allowing the denotations of the characters to shift in the pursuit of typographical ease. Finally, it is specific to the needs of Americanists rather than intendedly universal, seeking to provide characters for sounds routinely encountered in American languages, rather than to achieve universal coverage.

The American tradition emphasizes "compositionality" in symbolizations much more than the IPA system does. The basic vowel symbols of the system were patterned after Sweet's, but they were supplemented not by new characters but by diacritics which indicated reversal of backness (the umlaut), centrality (the over-dot), and so on. Compositionality is also seen in the consonant system, where sounds at cardinal points of articulation are defined and retraction and advancement diacritics (the under-dot and subscript arch respectively) are employed to represent nearby articulation points. Notice also the recommendations of Herzog et al. (1934) that the wedge diacritic should be used as an invariant indicator of palato-alveolar articulation. Explanation of these and other points in American and Americanist transcription are documented in the various entries in the guide. We have made brief mention of some relevant points here in order to give those familiar with American phonetic transcription an indication of our selection criteria for "American usage," and to make those unfamiliar with it aware that it is not a random set of variations from the IPA.

TONE TRANSCRIPTION

The organization of this book favors symbols for segmental transcription at the expense of notations for suprasegmental phenomena of tone and intonation. We have dealt with the common use of grave and acute accents, wedges, circumflexes, and breves as indicators of stress and tone in their entries. In doing so, we have presented the recommendations of *Principles* and the published American recommendations, though they leave quite a wide margin for variation. It is interesting, for example, to note the variation in the sample transcriptions of tone languages in *Principles,* nearly all of which alter the interpretations of the recommended symbols to suit the needs of each new language.

The transcription system chosen for tonal and intonational phenomena, either in a given language or for general use, reflects the phonological theory that underlies that system. As general theories of tone and intonation have developed, transcription practices have changed. We have not attempted to generalize across all of this variation, or to anticipate the directions in which currently emerging theories of the domain will lead.

THE MEDIA OF TRANSCRIPTION

Throughout this guide the reader will encounter metacomments about typography. Behind these there is a general point that merits some attention: the effect of medium on transcription. The primary media that are relevant are handwriting, typesetting, typing, and computer word processing.

Many works dealing with phonetic transcription (e.g. *Principles*, 53; Gleason 1955, 8; Smalley 1963, 232) rightly give attention to how phonetic symbols are to be written clearly and easily by hand. It is easy to see why. Linguistic or anthropological field work is one of the primary situations in which phonetic transcriptions are generated, and virtually all field notes are made in handwriting. The handwritten medium may well influence preferences for notation: the 'Polish hook' may seem faster to write as a nasal vowel diacritic than the superscript tilde; the subscript dot may be a clearer way of marking a retroflex consonant than the lengthened tail of the IPA symbol, and so on.

In the context of typesetting, entirely different considerations come to the fore. Designing new characters is an expensive business if it means contracting with a printer's shop to have new molds made from artists' drawings, and hundreds of new pieces of type cast in lead. The economic pressure to use an easily available diacritic combination, or to substitute a letter from an already available font, may be very strong. At the very least, prior availability of a character (e.g. in the Greek alphabet) or the fact that an easy modification can generate the character (e.g. turning an ⟨e⟩ to get a schwa) may loom as a large consideration in getting a particular transcriptional usage embedded in general practice.

Typing on a typewriter is different again. Turning a letter is very difficult (though perfectionists may recall having tried taking the paper out of the typewriter and re-inserting it upside down to get schwa and inverted *v* and the like), but other things, like back-up and overstrike, are very easy, and new conventions become practical: putting a hyphen through a letter to indicate spirantization of a stop or centralization of a vowel, for example.

Finally, the medium of the future: word processing on computing machines. Here standards like the ASCII (American Standard Code for Information Interchange) signal set may have to be reckoned with: the tilde and the circumflex have a place in the ASCII scheme but the wedge and the umlaut do not. However, more and more power to break away from inventories of pre-set symbols and into the creative designing of new characters and fonts is being made available by modern software and hardware. This technology brings greatly enhanced capabilities within reach. The production of the manuscript of this book would have been quite impossible for us without the equipment we used (an Apple Macintosh™ computer and Laserwriter™ printer, both from Apple) and the associated software (MacWrite™ and Mac-Draw™ from Apple, and Mac the Linguist™ from Megatherium Enterprises). But the medium also brings new freedom to deviate without limit and in unpredictable ways from every convention and style that has gone before. The freedom that a few influential figures like Sir Isaac Pitman and George Bernard Shaw had to devise and promulgate their own writing systems in printed form is fast becoming available to everyone. This may in due course introduce new complexities into the task of interpreting published phonetic transcriptions.

HOW TO FIND THINGS

This book has been organized, as far as possible, so that simply from the look of a symbol the user will be able to track it down quickly. If the symbol sought looks anything like a letter of the roman alphabet as used for English, it will be found where the English alphabetical order would suggest. Letters from other alphabets have been interpolated into the ordering either according to the sounds they represent (after roman letters which represent similar sounds, for example) or according to their shape, whichever seemed the most natural. Characters which are modifications of an ordinary letter are placed after that letter but before the next. More radical modifications follow less radical modifications, with turning (rotation through 180°) considered a particularly radical modification, and digraphic combination (as in ⟨æ⟩) even more so. Leafing through the book and glancing down the table of entries should give the user a good idea of the resulting arrangement fairly rapidly: variants of *a*, including α and *æ*, then variants of *A*, then variants of *b* and *B*, then β, then variants of *c*, and so on in what we hope is just the order you would have guessed we would use.

We have included cross-referencing guides at points where we felt a tension between ordering by denotation and ordering by form (though in fact these are rare; there are less than two dozen cross-references in the book). Ordering by form (as in a dictionary) penalizes the reader who is working from a preliminary general idea of a symbol's denotation but does not know its form (the problem that a poor speller has with standard dictionaries: you must be able to spell a word before you can look it up); but we have devised this guide primarily for use by someone who has *seen* a symbol and needs to determine what sound it probably was used to denote, so we have been able to organize by form to a very large extent. When we do order entries by denotation (as in a thesaurus), we face a different problem: where to find a completely alien character you have seen when you have no idea of its denotation.

Our solution has been to insert cross-references at points where we believe one might plausibly look on the basis of form, but where we have chosen to follow denotation instead. For example, the entry for *Barred o* (θ) will in fact be found with the *o*'s (because of what it stands for), but a cross-reference will be found in the entry for *Theta* (θ) (because it looks rather like a small theta, and looking for it near θ would be quite sensible).

In some cases, we followed denotation because it seemed to us that ordering by form would actually be perverse. In the specific case of symbols from the Greek alphabet, we decided always to place them after the entries for the English letters they are most obviously analogous to. Thus *Gamma* (γ) is placed after the symbols based on *g* because we feel most users naturally connect it with *g*, and not with variants of *y*, despite the (misleading) visual similarity. Likewise, because *Theta* is fairly well known to represent what *th* usually represents in English, it has been placed after the symbols related to *t*, not after *Capital o* on the strength of a rough visual similarity. (We actually resorted to informant work to confirm that this was the more intuitive thing to do.) We only deviate from this general strategy for Greek letters in two cases, namely *Eta* (η) and *Small Capital Delta* (Δ). Eta is placed after the variants of *n,* and Small Capital Delta is at the end of the symbols based on Capital A, because the usage of these (rare) symbols in phonetic transcriptions is based solely on their visual resemblances and not at all on what they stand for in Greek.

MAJOR AND MINOR ENTRIES

There are two types of entry: major and minor. Major entries always begin a new page. We have given a major entry to every character which is an officially recommended IPA character, and also to all those which we have judged to be standard symbols in current American transcriptional practice.

Interspersed among the major entries are the minor entries. These are reserved for characters which have less importance, either because they have been seriously proposed and occasionally used but have not gained wide currency, or because they are simply compositions of characters and diacritics whose interpretations are computable from the meanings of the components, and thus naturally fit in as addenda to major entries.

ORGANIZATION OF ENTRIES

At the head of each major entry, beside the large picture of the symbol is a convenient, though not necessarily official, working name for it. We have sometimes been able to use already current standard names (Greek letters all have well-known names, for example), but in other cases we have invented names according to fairly straightforward conventions. For example, an *h* with a dash or hyphen through the upright near the top is called *Crossed h;* an *h* with a dash or hyphen through its body would be called *Barred h;* an *h* with an oblique stroke (solidus or slash) through it would be *Slashed h;* an *h* with the top bent over rightward like a hook is called *Hooktop h;* an *h* rotated till it is upside down is called *Turned h;* and so on.

We have been careful here to distinguish among *turned, inverted* and *reversed* characters. A turned character is one that has been rotated 180°. An inverted character is one that has been reflected through a horizontal midline (switching top and bottom). A reversed character is one that has been reflected through a vertical midline (switching left and right).

All entries begin with a section headed **IPA Usage,** even if the symbol in question is not used at all under the IPA's proposals. This part of the entry explains the officially sanctioned use according to *Principles* and later official revisions. (Both the IPA as an association and the International Phonetic Alphabet are referred to as the IPA; the ambiguity is never pernicious.) We consider this an important feature of the guide, for *Principles,* apart from not being (at the time of publication) an up-to-date record of the IPA's position, was never designed as a reference guide (there is no index of symbols, for example). We hope to have provided here a more organized form of access to the large amount of information included in pages of *Principles* and elsewhere in the IPA's publications.

The next section in each entry is headed **American Usage.** This section attempts to do two things: first, to summarize a kind of informally standardized American usage that goes back ultimately to Boas and Sapir and is generally adhered to in such journals as *Language* or the *International Journal of American Linguistics;* and second, to mention uses of symbols proposed in the most influential American texts on articulatory phonetics and to explain how these proposals differ from the IPA's recommendations.

If there are further ways in which the symbol is employed, a section headed **Other Uses** follows.

Additional details that need to be pointed out about the symbol or what it stands for will be in a section headed **Comments** after that.

Finally, we provide a section titled **Source** in all the major entries. The information in this section is not meant to be paleographic. It includes two types of information: (a) an indication of the history of the character if that might help in suggesting a mnemonic for its transcriptional use, and (b) significant typographical information about the character.

NOTATIONAL MATTERS

We have distinguished carefully between references to symbols, letters, sounds, and symbols as used to transcribe sounds. When we refer to a symbol in its own right, e.g. to make a point about its shape, we put it in angled brackets thus: 'the symbol with the shape ⟨z⟩'. When we refer to a letter in a widely known alphabet like the Roman one, we italicize the letter thus: 'the letter *z*'. When we refer to a sound, we use a transcription of it according to the principles of the IPA, enclosed in square brackets. To forestall possible ambiguity we occasionally prefix the square brackets with the letters IPA thus: 'the voiced alveolar fricative, IPA [z]'. When we refer to a transcription according to a particular set of conventions, for example, the American conventions, we again use square brackets surrounding a symbol, and sometimes add quotation marks if it would make our intent clearer, thus: 'The transcription "[z]" means the same under American conventions as it does in the IPA system'. The only other thing square brackets are used for is to enclose occasional mentions of phonetic or phonological feature specifications, e.g. [+voice]; it is always clear from the context that these are not phonetic transcriptions, because although the plus sign and the minus sign have both been used as transcription symbols (see entries), they are postfixed to other symbols, and never appear as the first symbol in a transcribed form.

CHARTS

At the end of the book are a number of charts of symbols. The first two show the Cardinal Vowel system developed by Daniel Jones as a set of reference points for calibrating vowels articulatorily and auditorily. The next two show a fuller set of vowel symbols in the IPA tradition on charts of the same layout as the Cardinal Vowel charts, one for unrounded vowels and the other for rounded vowels.

Next are three charts of vowel symbols in the American tradition. The first is Bloch and Trager's. The second is a simplification of it that lacks Bloch and Trager's symmetry but has the advantage of roughly corresponding to most American practice today. The third is further simplified and corresponds to the tradition established by Chomsky and Halle (1968).

The remaining charts show consonant symbols. First we display the officially sanctioned consonant symbols of the IPA as of the 1979 revised chart (though we use what we think is an improved and more accurate layout). Then we give a chart of similar scope and layout for the American tradition, which, we should stress, we have at many points made maximally distinct from the IPA by deliberately giving possible American usages with the *Under-dot* diacritic for retraction (p. 212) and the *Subscript Arch* diacritic for fronting (p. 230), rather than their IPA equivalents (though the IPA symbols have also been used by American linguists).

We do not intend to suggest that the non-IPA usages in our American consonant chart *ought* to be used by American linguists. Quite the contrary: we suggest that the IPA prejudice against diacritics is well founded, and that it will generally be good policy to use the IPA's distinctive consonant symbols as fully as media restrictions permit. From this standpoint, our chart represents a standardization of a set of maximal divergences from the IPA system, and not at all a recommendation for such divergence. To guard against confusion arising from the mixing of traditions, we have not used ⟨c⟩ or ⟨j⟩ at all in the American chart. The entries for these symbols make it clear that they have no codifiable place in American transcription.

It is perhaps unavoidable that by supplying such charts we should be seen as having made a set of implicit recommendations. As we have said, this was not our intention in constructing them, but for those who will be looking at least for advice from what we have put into our charts, we would stress the following points.

First, the charts do not include anything like all the symbols in the book; we have deliberately avoided cluttering them with rarities, idiosyncrasies, exotica, digraphs, and representations for finer distinctions than linguists usually make.

Second, they do not include a place for every type of speech sound attested in languages. For an effort to classify the entire range of sounds found in a sample of 317 of the roughly four thousand languages in the world, the reader should consult Maddieson (1984), noting that Maddieson must use combinations of up to six characters and diacritics to represent some sounds (and his segment inventory is not exhaustive; languages with the bilabial click, IPA [⊙], happen to be absent from his sample).

Third, our charts do not attempt to list all the possibilities derivable by means of diacritic modification. The diacritics section of the book (pp. 204ff) should be consulted in this regard. For example, our IPA consonant chart shows no IPA symbols for dental stops, because, as is well known, the IPA convention is to use symbols like ⟨t⟩ and ⟨d⟩ (which we arbitrarily label as "Alveolar"), marking them with the *Subscript Bridge* diacritic (p. 206) if it is necessary to distinguish dentals from aveolars.

Fourth, and finally, the charts do not come with a guarantee. It is not necessarily the case that a transcription done by reference to the charts we provide here will be fully acceptable for its purpose. The most we can say is that our IPA charts set out the alphabet sanctioned by the world's most important international authority for phonetics, and that with regard to the American tradition, a transcription done by reference to our charts for American vowel and consonant representation, taking careful note of the information to be found in the entries for the symbols, is likely to be found acceptable for publication in most American linguistics and phonetics journals, and will probably not cause readers unnecessary puzzlement.

Puzzlement can always arise, however, in the difficult business of recording human speech in terms of a uniform, discrete alphabet. We can think of only one way to guard against it completely. It is very simple and obvious. When linguistic transcriptions are presented, they should be accompanied by a note stating clearly which transcription system has been used, with detailed notes on any unusual or potentially ambiguous symbols. If the publishers of books and journals in linguistics and phonetics chose to publish with their style sheets a detailed and carefully typeset chart showing the alphabet that they preferred, that would be even better. In the meantime, failing an industry-wide standard, each phonetician or linguist is an independent authority. We hope this book will be of use as a reference aid to guide those authorities in making their decisions.

Phonetic Symbol Guide

LOWER-CASE A

IPA USAGE

Cardinal vowel No. 4: low front unrounded. Described in *Principles* (p. 8) as the vowel sound of Northern English *back* or Parisian French *patte*. In the speech of Chicago, Illinois (and in various other varieties of American English), a word like *pop* is pronounced as IPA [pap]. In the speech typical of Boston, Massachusetts, the pronunciation of the word *park* is approximately [pɑːk].

AMERICAN USAGE

Same as IPA for many writers (see e.g. Bloch and Trager 1942, 22; Pike 1947, 5; Smalley 1963, 263; etc.); but many American linguists (see e.g. Gleason 1955, 8; Chomsky and Halle 1968) do not distinguish [a] from [ɑ], either one being used for any low unrounded vowel distinct from [æ], the choice depending on typographical considerations. Thus in some American writings, [a] is used as a low back unrounded vowel, as in *pop,* which is IPA [pɑp] in many American dialects, but may be transcribed [pap]. In Crothers (1978, 137) it is used for a low central vowel, IPA [ɐ].

OTHER USES

Universally used by Indologists for the short mid (or lower-mid) central unrounded vowel of Indic languages such as Hindi. Thus, for example, Fairbanks and Misra (1966) write ⟨kab⟩ for the Hindi word meaning 'when', IPA [kəb] or [kɐb].

COMMENTS

While many American linguists refer to [æ] as a low front vowel, the IPA and most careful American authorities are in agreement that [æ] represents a vowel slightly higher than fully low (between Cardinal 3 and Cardinal 4), while IPA [a] is defined as the lowest possible front vowel (Cardinal 4).

3

The IPA's effort to establish ⟨a⟩ and ⟨ɑ⟩ as separate symbols "has not met with the success originally hoped for" (*Principles,* 19). The fluent reader of roman letters is too accustomed to ignoring the difference between them when switching between fonts or between handwriting and printing or typing. No orthography has adopted the two symbols as contrasting letters, though they are used as contrasting symbols in Isaac Pitman's 1845 Phonotypic alphabet (cf. Pitman and St. John 1969, 82) and some dictionary pronunciation guides.

SOURCE
Roman alphabet, lower case (as usually found in printer's fonts and typewriter elements).

A with Over-dot

IPA Usage: Not used. *American Usage:* Not in general use. Following the recommendations of Boas et al. (1916, 10) for the use of an over-dot as a diacritic for central vowels, used by Bloch and Trager (1942, 22) for a low unrounded central vowel, approximately IPA [ɐ̞]. *Comments:* It is used for a low central *rounded* vowel in Crothers (1978, 137), where '[a]' is used for Bloch and Trager's [ȧ].

A Umlaut

IPA Usage: According to *Principles* (p. 16), a low central unrounded vowel, though the current interpretation of the umlaut diacritic (q.v.) makes it a low central*ized* front unrounded vowel. *American Usage:* According to the widely followed recommendation of Boas et al.

(1916, 9) on the use of the umlaut (q.v.) with vowel symbols, if [a] is a low back vowel, [ä] would be a low front unrounded vowel, i.e. IPA [a] (or perhaps [æ]). Used in this sense in Crothers (1978, 137). Where [a] is used for a low front unrounded vowel (e.g. Bloch and Trager 1942, 22), [ä] is a low back unrounded vowel. The symbol is not in common use, but is occasionally found. *Comments:* The result of the change in the IPA's interpretation of the umlaut and its common use with a different sense in American practice is a rather confusing situation in which [ä] may denote a centralized front vowel (official IPA), a central vowel (*Principles*), or a back vowel (e.g. Bloch and Trager).

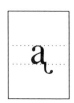

Right-hook A

IPA Usage: Recommended in *Principles* (p. 14) for a vowel with the quality of [a] (i.e. Cardinal 4) with rhotacization (*r*-coloration). Approval of the right-hook diacritic (q.v.) was withdrawn in 1976 (*Journal of the International Phonetic Association* [*JIPA*] 6, 3) in favor of a digraph such as [aɹ] or [aˈ]. *American Usage:* Not used. *Comments:* The rightward hook used by the IPA for indicating rhotacization should not be confused with the centered "Polish hook"; for example, ⟨ą⟩ is used in Polish orthography and Americanist (e.g. Smalley 1963, 333) transcription for nasalized vowels.

TURNED A

IPA USAGE

A not quite fully open, central unrounded vowel; higher than Cardinal 4, lower than Cardinal 3. Illustrated by the unstressed short open final syllable in British English words such as *sofa,* pronounced [sə ω fɐ].

AMERICAN USAGE

Not used.

COMMENTS

This symbol is rather rare in practice. None of the editions of Gimson's *Introduction to the Pronunciation of English* (1962, 1970, 1980) use it, for example.

SOURCE

Roman alphabet lower-case ⟨a⟩, turned (rotated 180°).

SCRIPT A

Cardinal vowel No. 5: low back unrounded.

AMERICAN USAGE

Standardly, same as IPA if used; but for many linguists not distinct from ⟨a⟩, either being used for any low unrounded vowel distinct from [æ], the choice depending on type font, and thus usually ⟨a⟩ when printed or typewritten.

Pike (1947, 5) and Smalley (1963, 174) show [ɑ] for a low *central* unrounded vowel. Pike has no symbol for a low back unrounded vowel, and Smalley proposes ⟨ɒ⟩ (rather misleadingly; see the entry for *Turned Script A*).

COMMENTS

The IPA's effort to establish ⟨ɑ⟩ and ⟨a⟩ as separate symbols "has not met with the success originally hoped for" (*Principles*, 19). The fluent reader of roman letters is too accustomed to ignoring the difference between them. No orthography has adopted the two symbols as contrasting letters, though they are used as contrasting symbols in Isaac Pitman's 1845 Phonotypic alphabet (cf. Pitman and St. John 1969, 82) and some dictionary pronunciation guides.

SOURCE

Roman alphabet lower-case *a* as handwritten.

Lower-case Alpha

IPA Usage: Not used. *American Usage:* Boas et al. (1916, 2) recommend ⟨α⟩ to represent the vowel sound in English *but,* classifying it as an upper-mid back unrounded vowel. It is sometimes found as a typographical substitute for script *a,* ⟨ɑ⟩; see e.g. Smalley 1963 where alpha is used to denote a low central unrounded vowel. Smalley refers to it as (written *a* or) script *a* (p. 261), showing clearly that a typographical compromise is involved. It is used in Crothers (1978, 137) for a low back rounded vowel (IPA [ɒ]). *Source:* Taken from the Greek alphabet, lower case.

TURNED SCRIPT A

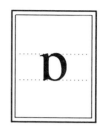

Cardinal vowel No. 13: low back rounded. The secondary cardinal vowel corresponding to Cardinal 5.

AMERICAN USAGE

Standardly, same as IPA if used (cf. Pike 1947, 5); but Smalley (1963, 261) regards the vowel in question as *un*rounded, IPA [ɑ] (rounding is all but neutralized for very low vowels), and many linguists do not use the symbol at all, using [ɑ] or [a] for low back unrounded vowels and open *o* (i.e. ⟨ɔ⟩) for low back rounded vowels.

The transcription system of Kurath 1939 (p. 126) seeks to remedy variation in use of the turned script *a* for both unrounded and rounded low back vowels (e.g. by Bernard Bloch) through the use of a reversed turned script *a* to unambiguously represent an unrounded low back vowel, turned script *a* being reserved for rounded vowels.

COMMENTS

The IPA (*Principles*, 7–9) distinguishes between a fully open, fully back vowel with lip rounding, as in Southern British English *hot* (/hɒt/), and a slightly closer vowel, as in Southern British *caught* (/kɔːt/) or the Scottish pronunciation of *hot* (/hɔt/). Because American dialects generally do not show a /ɔ/-/ɒ/ phonological distinction (and even in Southern British there is a concomitant length difference), the need for both symbols is not felt by many American linguists.

SOURCE

Roman alphabet lower-case *a* as handwritten, turned (rotated 180°).

Turned Script A with Over-dot

IPA Usage: Not used. *American Usage:* Not in general use, but following the recommendations of Boas et al. (1916, 10), used by Bloch and Trager (1942, 22) for a low central rounded vowel. Trager (1964, 16) suggests [ɐ] as an alternative (conflicting with the IPA definition of this symbol). The *Principles* transcription for a low central rounded vowel would be [ɒ̈], which Bloch and Trager use for a low front rounded vowel.

Turned Script A Umlaut

IPA Usage: According to *Principles* (p. 16), a low central rounded vowel, i.e. basically [ɒ+], though the current interpretation of the umlaut diacritic (q.v.) makes it a low central*ized* back rounded vowel. *American Usage:* According to the widely followed recommendation of Boas et al. (1916, 9) on the use of the umlaut (q.v.) with vowel symbols, if [ɒ] is taken to be a low back rounded vowel, [ɒ̈] would represent a low front rounded vowel, i.e. a vowel with all of the properties of [ɒ] but front instead of back. The IPA transcription would be [œ]. The symbol is not in general use, but is listed by Bloch and Trager (1942, 22). Trager (1964, 16) proposes a ligature of the small capitals ⟨ᴀ⟩ and ⟨ᴏ⟩ as an alternative symbol. *Comments:* The result of the change in the IPA's interpretation of the umlaut and its common use with a different sense in American practice is a rather confusing situation in which [ɒ̈] may denote a centralized back vowel (official IPA), a central vowel (*Principles*), or a front vowel (e.g. Bloch and Trager).

Reversed Turned Script A

The symbol is not in general use. Kurath (1939, 126) reports that some of the field workers for the *Linguistic Atlas of New England* (e.g. Bloch) had used turned script *a* (q.v.) indifferently for both rounded and unrounded low back vowels. This character was invented by analogy to unambiguously denote an unrounded low back vowel so that turned script *a* could be reserved for a rounded low back vowel in future work. Extremely rare.

ASH

IPA USAGE

A not quite fully open, front unrounded vowel; higher than Cardinal 4 (IPA [a]), lower than Cardinal 3 (IPA [ɛ]). Illustrated by *Principles* (p. 9) with Southern British English *cat* ([kæt]) and Russian *pjat'* ('five').

AMERICAN USAGE

Standardly, same as IPA. Many American linguists refer to [æ] as a low front vowel. See e.g. Gleason (1955, 8), Chomsky and Halle (1968, 176), Halle and Mohanan (1985, 57). However, many American works on phonetics, e.g. Bloch and Trager (1942, 22), Pike (1947, 5), and Maddieson (1984, 251), are in agreement with the IPA in using [æ] to represent a vowel slightly higher than fully low ("higher-low," "raised low," etc.). Smalley (1963, 263) reconciles the American terminology with the IPA usage by calling [æ] "low" and [a] "lower-low."

SOURCE

Taken from Old English orthography, where the *a-e* ligature was used to represent the sound of the runic symbol with the mnemonic name *æsc* 'ash'. The upper-case form is ⟨Æ⟩. The letter is used occasionally in modern English printing for certain words of Latin origin (e.g. *formulæ* and *encyclopædia*), though it does not represent [æ] in these words.

Ash with Over-dot

IPA Usage: Not used. *American Usage:* Not in general use. Following the recommendations of Boas et al. (1916, 10) for the use of an over-dot as a diacritic for central vowels, used by Bloch and Trager (1942, 22) for a higher-low unrounded central vowel, approximately IPA[ɐ]. It is used with this sense in Crothers (1978, 137).

Ash Umlaut

IPA Usage: According to *Principles* (p. 16), a higher-low central unrounded vowel, between Cardinals 3 and 4 in height and between Cardinals 3 and 6 in backness, similar to [ɐ]. The current interpretation of the umlaut diacritic (q.v.) makes it a low central*ized* front unrounded vowel, between [æ] and [ɐ]. *American Usage:* According to the widely followed recommendation of Boas et al. (1916, 9) on the use of the umlaut (q.v.) with vowel symbols, this would represent a vowel with all of the properties of [æ] but back instead of front. Trager (1964, 16) suggests [ä] or [ʌ] as alternative transcriptions for such a vowel. The symbol is rarely found. The IPA would use [ʌ−] or [ɑ+] for Bloch and Trager's [ä]. *Comments:* The change in the IPA's interpretation of the umlaut and its common use with a different sense in American practice has resulted in a rather confusing situation in which [ä] with the umlaut diacritic may denote a centralized front vowel (official IPA), a central vowel (*Principles*), or a back vowel (Bloch and Trager).

A-O Ligature

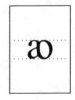

IPA Usage: Not used.   *American Usage:* Proposed by Trager (1964, 16) for a higher-low front rounded vowel, an alternative to the transcription [ö] suggested by Bloch and Trager (1942, 22). A Trager suggestion that never caught on. Front rounded vowels lower than IPA [œ] are in any case essentially unattested, though the IPA now provides [ɶ] for a low front rounded vowel.

SMALL CAPITAL A

IPA USAGE

Not sanctioned. *JIPA* (5, 52) mentions it as having been proposed, and occasionally used, as a symbol for a fully open central unrounded vowel.

AMERICAN USAGE

No standard use, but used in various ways by early Americanists, especially in the *Handbook of American Indian Languages* (Boas 1911). Thus Jones (1911, 744) uses ⟨ᴀ⟩ for IPA [ʌ], and Thalbitzer (1911, 975) uses it for "uvularized ɑ," i.e. [ɑ] when adjacent to a uvular consonant. The recommendations of Boas et al. (1916, 10) concerning the use of small capital letters would make ⟨ᴀ⟩ the transcription of a voiceless [a].

SOURCE

Roman alphabet, small capital font.

Capital A

IPA Usage: Not used.   *American Usage:* Boas et al. (1916, 10) recommend the use of small capitals to represent the voiceless versions of normally voiced sounds (either vowels or sonorants), and following this, Pike (1947, 5) and Smalley (1963, 392) both use a general convention of capital letters for voiceless vowels; thus the transcription [A] might be used for IPA [ḁ].   *Other uses:* Used also in various ways in phonological work. For example, *A* represents the morphophoneme proposed by Hamp (1951) as the trigger of the initial consonant mutation Aspiration in Old Irish and Welsh. It represents an *a*-coloring laryngeal in some Indo-Europeanist work (see Hamp 1965a, 123, n. 3). And in Chomsky and Halle (1968, chaps. 2−4) it is used to represent informally the vocalic nucleus that is realized as [æ] when lax and [ey] when tense.

Inverted Small Capital A

IPA Usage: Not used.   *American Usage:* Not in use, but proposed by Trager (1964, 16) to represent a higher low central unrounded vowel, as an alternative to the transcription [æ̇] suggested by Bloch and Trager (1942, 22). Trager suggests that [ᴀ] should be used for a back unrounded vowel that is "higher low" (between Cardinal 5 and 6) and [ʋ] should be used for the corresponding central vowel. The suggestion apparently never caught on.

Capital Ash

IPA Usage: Not used.   *American Usage:* Boas et al. (1916, 10) recommend the use of small capitals to represent the voiceless versions of normally voiced sounds (either vowels or sonorants) and following this, Pike (1947, 5) and Smalley (1963, 392) both use a general convention of capital letters for voiceless vowels; thus the transcription [Æ] might be used for IPA [æ̥].   *Comments:* The upper-case version of the *a-e* ligature with the mnemonic name *æsc* 'ash'.

Small Capital A-O Ligature

IPA Usage: Not used. *American Usage:* Not in use, but proposed by Trager (1964, 16) for a low front rounded vowel, as an alternative to the transcription [ɒ] suggested by Bloch and Trager (1942, 22). *Comments: Principles* does not give a symbol for representing a vowel of the sort this symbol was intended for. Chomsky and Halle (1968, 191–92) used [œ] for it. In 1976 the IPA added ⟨Œ⟩ to its chart of secondary vowel symbols (*JIPA* 6, 2) for a low front rounded vowel. Such vowels are essentially unattested in natural languages, so none of these symbols are used in practice.

INVERTED V

Cardinal vowel No. 14: lower-mid back unrounded; but see comments below. The secondary cardinal vowel corresponding to Cardinal 6.

AMERICAN USAGE

Same as IPA, if used. Some variation of range is encountered; see comments below.

COMMENTS

The IPA transcription [ʌ] was initially defined to represent the fully back Cardinal 14, but one of its most common uses is for representing the vowel sound of Southern British English *cup*. Most descriptions agree that this sound is central rather than back. *Principles* (p. 9) makes the very misleading remark that [ʌ] can be heard in Northern England pronunciations of *cup*, but *cup* is often pronounced [kʊp] in Northern England.

Caution should be exercised in interpreting uses of [ʌ] and [ə] in American works. The symbol is used by Bloch and Trager (1942, 22) in its IPA sense, lower-mid back. Pike (1947, 5) considers it lower-mid central and Smalley (1963, 363) gives it as low (higher than his "lower-low" series) central.

There is no phonological distinction between [ʌ] and [ə] in many American dialects, and American linguists often treat the two symbols as interchangeable (see e.g. the confusing note provided by Cartier and Todaro 1983, 17). Gleason (1955) does not use it. The chart of segment types in Chomsky and Halle (1968, 176) shows [ʌ] as a mid vowel ([-high, -low, +back, -round, -tense]). This apparently does not allow for it to be distinguished phonetically from schwa (q.v., p. 44).

Roman alphabet lower-case v, vertically inverted. Visually suggestive of the small capital ⟨A⟩ without a crossbar, thus perhaps hinting at a low back tongue position. Note that ⟨ʌ⟩ is not the same as either ⟨Λ⟩ (upper-case Greek lambda) or ⟨∧⟩ (logical conjunction), though not all typesetters have appreciated this; the Mohawk transcriptions in Postal (1964), for example, contain numerous inverted *v*'s wrongly set as logical conjunction signs. Inverted *v* is often called "wedge," and sometimes (incorrectly) called "caret."

Small Capital Delta

IPA Usage: Not used. *American Usage:* Not in use, but proposed by Trager (1964, 16) to represent a mid back unrounded vowel, as an alternative to the transcription [E] suggested by Bloch and Trager (1942, 22). A Trager suggestion that never caught on. The reason for the choice of symbol may have been the visual similarity between ⟨Δ⟩, ⟨ʌ⟩, and ⟨A⟩. *Source:* A small capital from the Greek alphabet. It is used in syntactic literature as a dummy terminal symbol, but not generally as a phonetic symbol.

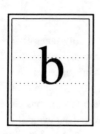

LOWER-CASE B

IPA USAGE

Voiced bilabial stop.

AMERICAN USAGE

Same as IPA.

COMMENTS

Not always used for a phonetically voiced stop; in languages like Mandarin Chinese and Icelandic, it may be used in broad transcription or in orthography for an unaspirated voiceless stop that contrasts with an aspirated one.

SOURCE

Roman alphabet, lower case.

Underdot B

IPA Usage: Not used. *American Usage:* Used by Trager (1964, 22) to represent a labiodental stop (an alternative to his ⟨ɓ⟩), following the general recommendation of Boas et al. (1916, 10) of underdot as a retraction sign for consonants. The symbol is hardly ever used, not least because labiodental stops seem never to contrast with bilabial stops in any language.

Crossed B

Widely used by Indo-Europeanists, e.g. Brugmann (1904; see p. 1 for his symbol chart), Prokosch (1939, 35 etc.), Wright (1910, 54 etc.), for a voiced bilabial fricative ("spirant"), IPA [β], and also in Romance philology; see e.g. the transcriptions in Quilis and Vaquero (1973) or Fontanals (1976).

Barred B

IPA Usage: Not used. *American Usage:* Not standard; but used by Pike and Smalley for a voiced bilabial fricative (IPA [β]), and still sometimes found: see e.g. the transcriptions in Danesi (1982). *Comments:* By a general convention, barred stop symbols (with a superimposed hyphen or short dash through the body of the letter) are often used to represent those fricatives for which the IPA symbols are not used. The resultant symbols have the advantage of being easy to type on an unmodified typewriter. The symbol is used with this sense by Meillet and Cohen (1952, xiii).

Slashed B

Occasionally found for a voiced bilabial fricative, IPA [β], as a typographical variant of barred or crossed *b;* see e.g. Joos (1966,

400–404), where the crossed *b* of an earlier source is reset in a way looking more like a slashed *b*.

Soft Sign

IPA Usage: Not used. *American Usage:* Not used. *Other uses:* Used for the Indo-European "shva secundum," the reduction of a short vowel, in contrast to [ə], the "shva primum," the reduction of a long vowel (Prokosch 1939, 94). Also used by Hamp (see e.g. 1965b, 225) for a postulated sixth vowel in Proto-Keltic. *Source:* The character is taken from the Cyrillic alphabet. In Russian orthography, the soft sign indicates that the preceding consonant has a palatal articulation.

Hard Sign

IPA Usage: Not used. *American Usage:* Proposed by Trager (1964, 16) to represent a lower high back unrounded vowel; an alternative to ⟨ï⟩. *Source:* Taken from the Cyrillic alphabet, lower case. In Bulgarian orthography, the hard sign corresponds to a vowel of similar quality to the one that the symbol denotes in the Trager system, which may have been the motivation for this choice. The symbol has seldom if ever been used in phonetic work.

HOOKTOP B

IPA USAGE

Glottalic ingressive (i.e. implosive) bilabial stop.

AMERICAN USAGE

Same as IPA, except that Trager (1964, 22) idiosyncratically proposes this symbol for a (pulmonic egressive) voiced labiodental stop.

COMMENTS

The IPA usage is well established, and since labiodental stops are not found contrasting with bilabial stops, Trager's suggestion has not gained any currency.

SOURCE

Roman alphabet lower-case ⟨b⟩, modified.

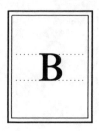

SMALL CAPITAL B

IPA USAGE

Not used.

AMERICAN USAGE

Not generally used. According to the recommendations of Boas et al. (1916, 10) on the use of small capitals, small capital *b* could be used for a labial stop "intermediate . . . between sonant and surd."

OTHER USES

Proposed by Ladefoged (1982, 154–55) for a bilabial trill (as represented by writers in the form "Brr," for complaining about the cold). This is reported by Ladefoged to occur as an "*r*-sound" in some Papua New Guinea and some African languages, and is reported to occur in the name of the ant lion (but in no other words!) in Amuzgo and Isthmus Zapotec (Suarez 1983, 46). Smalley (1963, 456) suggests *b* with superscript tilde for a bilabial trill; Suarez writes [b'], following the IPA's suggestion that "small index letters may be used to indicate shades of sound" (*Principles,* p. 17).

SOURCE

Roman alphabet, small capital font.

BETA

IPA USAGE

Voiced bilabial fricative.

AMERICAN USAGE

Same as IPA, if used; *Barred b,* ⟨ɓ⟩, *Crossed b,* ⟨ƀ⟩, or occasionally *Slashed b,* ⟨ƀ⟩ (q.v.) may be found instead.

COMMENTS

As in Spanish *iba* 'was (3rd singular)'. Contrasts with labiodental [v] in some languages, e.g. Avatime, Ewe, and Logba in the Kwa group in West Africa (see Ladefoged 1968, 25).

SOURCE

Greek alphabet, lower case.

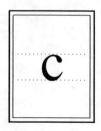

LOWER-CASE C

IPA USAGE

Voiceless palatal stop. As represented by *ty* in Hungarian orthography.

AMERICAN USAGE

Sometimes as IPA, but since 1934, commonly used for an alveolar affricate, IPA [ts], following the recommendations of Herzog et al. (1934, 631).

Recommended by Boas et al. (1916, 5) for a voiceless palato-alveolar fricative, IPA [ʃ], but this was supplanted by the later recommendations of Herzog et al. that [š] be used for [ʃ] and [c] be reserved for [ts] in those cases where it functioned as a single affricate consonant. Smalley (1963, 275) uses it for a voiceless alveopalatal stop.

OTHER USES

Boas 1911 (p. 23) gives [c] for a voiceless "dental" fricative, though it is given as "alveolar" in his Chinook paper (p. 565). Jones (1911, 743) uses it for IPA [ʃ]. The variation may be as much in descriptive terminology as denotation. The most likely use of unadorned ⟨c⟩ in this period is for some voiceless coronal fricative.

Indologists use ⟨c⟩ for the palato-alveolar affricates of such languages as Hindi as well as for true palatal stops (and generally refer to such consonants as 'palatals' even if they are produced with palato-alveolar contact). Cf. Whitney (1889, 2).

COMMENTS

Hungarian *ty* represents IPA [c]. German *z* represents American [c] (=IPA [ts]).

Roman alphabet, lower case. It seldom denotes IPA [c] in the languages in whose orthographies it appears. It is fairly close in Italian *ciao*, and hence was a natural choice for scholars transliterating Sanskrit च .

C Acute

IPA Usage: Not used. *American Usage:* Proposed by Trager (1964, 22) to represent a voiceless prepalatal affricate; an alternative to Trager's [ç] (not the same as IPA [ç]). The IPA equivalent of Trager's [ç] = [ć] would be [tʃ] = [tʃʲ]. *Other uses:* Found in some European works with a similar denotation to the one Trager suggests; for instance, Trubetzkoy (1932, 38) uses ⟨ć⟩ for the affricate corresponding to palatalized ("mouillert") [s] which he writes with ⟨ś⟩. Since the prime, an acute accent placed after the symbol, [ʹ] is also used to indicate palatalization among American and continental European linguists, [cʹ] is likely to have a similar interpretation to [ć] when found. Also used in the Polish and Serbo-Croatian orthographies.

Barred C

IPA Usage: Not used. *American Usage:* Proposed by Smalley (1963, 455) for a voiceless flat (i.e. not grooved) "alveopalatal" (palato-alveolar) fricative. *Other uses:* The symbol is also used by Meillet and Cohen (1952, xiii) for a voiceless palatal fricative, the "*ich*-laut", presumably IPA [ç]. *Comments:* By a general convention, barred stop symbols (with a superimposed hyphen or short dash through the body of the letter) are often used to represent those fricatives for which the IPA symbols are not used. The resultant symbols have the advantage of being easy to type on an unmodified typewriter. Barred *c* is probably supposed to be equivalent to IPA [ç].

Slashed C

IPA Usage: Not used. *American Usage:* Voiceless alveolar or dental centrally released affricate (IPA [ts]). Used in both Gleason 1955 and Pike 1947. Note that some other sources (e.g. Herzog et al. [1934, 631], Hockett 1955) use ⟨c⟩ instead. *Other uses:* Used in Boas 1911 (p. 23) as a voiceless "linguo-dental" or "linguo-labial" [sic] fricative, a use supplanted by [θ] in later work. *Comments:* We have analyzed this character as a roman alphabet lowercase ⟨c⟩ with a superimposed oblique stroke. In some fonts the superimposed stroke is vertical rather than oblique, but this is never a distinctive feature of the symbol. An effectively equivalent symbol is usually available on American typewriter keyboards as the "cent sign." Its absence as a character on computer terminal keyboards and non-U.S. typewriters favors our decision to treat it as a *c* with a superimposed stroke.

C WEDGE

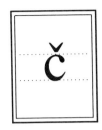

Not used.

AMERICAN USAGE

Voiceless palato-alveolar affricate, IPA [tʃ]. The recommendation of Herzog et al. (1934, 631) that [č] be used for IPA [tʃ] has gained almost universal currency among American linguists.

SOURCE

Roman alphabet lower-case *c*, with the wedge diacritic. As used in the orthography for Czech, where the diacritic is called the *haček* ('little hook').

C CEDILLA

IPA USAGE

Voiceless palatal central fricative. Articulated further back than [ʃ] (palato-alveolar) or [ç] ("alveolo-palatal") but not as far back as [x] (velar).

AMERICAN USAGE

Generally not used. Palatal fricatives are generally transcribed with symbols for fronted velar fricatives. Hence Pike (1947, 7) and Gleason (1955, 7) give [x̟] for a voiceless palatal central fricative, and Smalley (1963, 359) specifies [x̣].

COMMENTS

Illustrated by the initial segment of English *hue* in some pronunciations, by the final sound of German *ich,* and by the initial segment of Japanese *hito.*

Used in Boas 1911 (p. 23) as a voiced "linguo-dental" or "linguo-labial" [sic] fricative, a use supplanted by [ð] in later work.

The cedilla is used in French and formerly in Spanish to indicate a fricative value as opposed to a stop or affricate value for the letter *c* in contexts where the stop value would otherwise be expected. Thus in French, *c* = [k] in *cas* but [s] in *ça.* The letter *c* with a cedilla is also used in Turkish orthography, to denote a voiceless palato-alveolar affricate, IPA [tʃ]. Note that it does not actually denote a palatal fricative in any of these orthographic uses.

SOURCE

Roman alphabet lower-case *c* (used for a palatal stop), with the cedilla diacritic.

CURLY-TAIL C

IPA USAGE

Voiceless "alveolo-palatal" central laminal fricative. Articulated further forward than [ç] (true palatal) but not as far forward as [ʃ] (palato-alveolar), and articulated laminally (with the flat blade of the tongue) rather than apically (with the tip of the tongue, as in the retroflex [ʂ]).

AMERICAN USAGE

Not in general use. Listed in Halle and Clements (1983, 29) as a voiceless palatal central fricative, i.e. IPA [ç].

COMMENTS

Illustrated (*Principles,* 12) by the sound represented as *ś* in Polish *geś,* and as *hs* in the Wade romanization for Mandarin Chinese (*x* in the Pinyin system).

The IPA's distinction between "alveolo-palatal" place of articulation (closer to palatal) and palato-alveolar (closer to alveolar) has not gained wide currency. The term palato-alveolar is standard, but the term "alveolo-palatal" is not, and in fact is rarely encountered. The term "alveopalatal" used by Gleason, Pike, and Smalley corresponds to the IPA's palato-alveolar.

SOURCE

Roman alphabet lower-case *c* (used by IPA for a palatal stop), modified with the same curly tail used for ⟨ʑ⟩ (IPA's voiced "alveolo-palatal" central fricative).

STRETCHED C

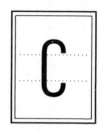

IPA USAGE

"Retroflex" click (i.e. velaric ingressive postalveolar stop); see comments below.

AMERICAN USAGE

Not normally used.

COMMENTS

Illustrated by the click that *q* represents in the Zulu orthography, which is generally referred to as "palatal" in the literature, but has also been called "retroflex," especially in earlier work.

The sound is similar to the pop of a cork being drawn from a bottle. It has been described by Ladefoged and Traill (1984, 2), after a careful investigation of the articulation, as *alveolar* rather than "retroflex" or "palatal." As they acknowledge (p. 6), this is a departure from earlier works, and may cause some confusion, since there is another click (written [≠] in the local orthography for Hottentot and by many linguists) that has been called alveolar but which Ladefoged and Traill claim is palatal. The difficulty apparently stems not so much from a disagreement about how the sound is made as from the conceptual problem of what should be called the primary place of articulation of a sound with velaric closure, apico-alveolar closure, and oral airflow into a palatal cavity.

Printed as ⟨C⟩ in some sources, e.g. Chomsky and Halle (1968, 320), and as ⟨ʗ⟩ in Beach (1938, 289). Beach gives [ʗ̧] for the nasalized version (p. 289).

SOURCE

Perhaps a visual compromise between ⟨c⟩ on the one hand and the rightward-swept tail of retroflex consonant symbols like ⟨ʈ⟩ and ⟨ɖ⟩ on the other.

Upper-case C

Sometimes found as a typographical compromise for [ɕ] (a palatal click); see e.g. Chomsky and Halle (1968, 320) and the occurrence of "Chū" for "ɕhū:" in the bibliography of Cole (1966, 470).

Also used by phonologists to represent an arbitrary consonant of any sort; thus "CV syllable structure" means "Consonant-Vowel syllable structure," and so on.

Open O
See page 117.

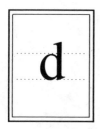

LOWER-CASE D

IPA USAGE

Voiced dental or alveolar stop. [d̪] indicates definitely dental; [d] may represent either articulation.

AMERICAN USAGE

Same as IPA.

COMMENTS

The exact place of articulation for an apical stop can be indicated with diacritics. For example, American phoneticians may mark dental articulation with a subscript arch (or the IPA bridge diacritic), and may indicate retroflex articulation with an underdot.

The symbol is not always used for a phonetically voiced stop; in languages like Mandarin Chinese and Icelandic, it may be used in broad transcription or in orthography for an unaspirated voiceless stop that contrasts with an aspirated one.

SOURCE

Roman alphabet, lower case.

Crossed D

IPA Usage: Not used. *American Usage:* Sometimes found representing a voiced interdental fricative, but standard American usage for this is [ð], as in IPA. *Other uses:* Widely used to represent a voiced interdental fricative in transliterations of early Germanic languages (e.g. by Wright [1910, 54] for Gothic and generally by Brugmann 1904; see p. 1 for his symbol chart). Also found in works on Romance linguistics; see e.g. the transcriptions in Quilis and Vaquero (1973), Fontanals (1976). Appears with this sense in Meillet and Cohen (1952, xiii). A typographical substitute for ⟨ð⟩, whose capital form is ⟨Đ⟩.

Barred D

IPA Usage: Not used. *American Usage:* Not standard, but sometimes used (e.g. by Pike [1947, 7] and Smalley [1963, 454]) for a voiced interdental fricative (IPA [ð]), and still sometimes found; see e.g. the transcriptions in Danesi (1982). *Comments:* Barred stop symbols (with a superimposed hyphen or short dash through the body of the letter) are often used to represent those fricatives for which the IPA symbols are not used. The resultant symbols have the advantage of being easy to type on an unmodified typewriter. In the case at hand, there is no difficulty in finding a suitable symbol for the voiced grooved alveolar fricative, since ⟨z⟩ is on every English-language typewriter; barred *d* provides a way of representing a dental or interdental slit (flat) fricative.

Slashed D

May occasionally be found for a voiced interdental fricative, IPA [ð], though we have not been able to locate a printed source.

D with Upper-left Hook

Used by Daniel Jones in early transcriptions to indicate a voiced retro-flex stop, in particular for Sinhalese. According to Jones, the IPA symbol [ɖ] was introduced in 1927 (see Jones and Laver 1973, 202, n. 36), replacing this character and the traditional [ḍ].

HOOKTOP D

IPA USAGE

Glottalic ingressive (i.e. implosive) alveolar or dental stop.

AMERICAN USAGE

Same as IPA.

COMMENTS

Dental vs. alveolar contrast can be shown by [ɖ̪] vs. [ɗ].

Smalley (1963) describes voiceless as well as voiced implosives and reserves ⟨ɗ⟩ for a voiced one. It appears, however, that implosives occurring in natural languages are nearly always voiced.

SOURCE

Roman alphabet lower-case *d*, modified.

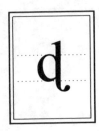

RIGHT-TAIL D

IPA USAGE

Voiced retroflex (i.e. apico-postalveolar) stop.

AMERICAN USAGE

Not normally used; [ɖ] is used instead.

COMMENTS

As in the sound represented by Hindi ⟨ ड ⟩.

SOURCE

Roman alphabet lower-case *d,* modified by the addition of the right-ward long tail used by the IPA for retroflex consonant symbols. Introduced in 1927, according to Daniel Jones (Jones and Laver 1973, 202, n. 36).

D-YOGH LIGATURE

IPA USAGE

Voiced palato-alveolar affricate.

AMERICAN USAGE

Not generally used; [dž] or [ǰ] would be used instead.

SOURCE

A ligature of ⟨d⟩ and ⟨ʒ⟩. A palato-alveolar affricate has an alveolar stop component (hence the ⟨d⟩) and a palato-alveolar fricative offglide (hence the ⟨ʒ⟩).

ETH

IPA USAGE

Voiced apico-dental or interdental central fricative.

AMERICAN USAGE

Same as IPA. Sometimes [ꝺ] or [đ] is found instead.

SOURCE

The letter *eth* originated in Old English orthography as a crossed Irish *d*. The symbols *thorn* (⟨þ⟩) and *eth* were used indifferently in Late Old English manuscripts to represent the interdental fricative phoneme which was voiced between two voiced sounds and voiceless elsewhere. Cf. Quirk and Wrenn (1957, 6–7). The character was borrowed for Scandinavian orthographies and survives in Modern Icelandic. The upper-case form is ⟨Đ⟩.

Lower-case Delta

Not generally used, but if found it is probably for a voiced interdental fricative, IPA [ð]. Cf. Sapir (1925, 43) and Firth (1948, 140).

Recommended by Boas et al. (1916, 11) for a voiced "dorsal" stop. Transcriptions using the symbols for such a dorsal series are seldom found.

Delta represents IPA [ð] in Modern Greek.

Small Capital Delta
See page 19.

CAPITAL D

IPA USAGE

Not used.

AMERICAN USAGE

Often used to represent the voiced alveolar flap of American pronunciations of words like *pity;* thus American [pɪDi] = IPA [pɪɾi]. Cf. Chomsky (1964, 90).

SOURCE

Roman alphabet, upper case.

LOWER-CASE E

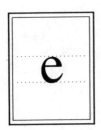

IPA USAGE

Cardinal Vowel No. 2: upper-mid front unrounded.

AMERICAN USAGE

Standardly, same as IPA; but commonly also used for Cardinal 3 (IPA [ɛ]). Thus in transcribing English, the mid vowel of *bait* may be distinguished from that of *bet* by length ([beːt] vs. [bet]) or diphthongization ([beyt] vs. [bet]—IPA [beit] or [beʊt] vs. [bɛt]).

SOURCE

The letter *e* is commonly a symbol for a vowel like Cardinal 2 in European languages (e.g. French, Spanish, and Italian).

E Umlaut

IPA Usage: According to *Principles* (p. 16), an upper-mid unrounded central vowel (between Cardinals 2 and 15 in backness, i.e. between [e] and [ɤ]). The current interpretation of the umlaut diacritic (q.v.) makes it a central*ized* upper-mid unrounded vowel. *American Usage:* According to the widely followed recommendation of Boas et al. (1916, 9) on the use of the umlaut (q.v.) with vowel symbols, [ë] would represent an unrounded higher-mid back vowel, i.e. a vowel with all of the properties of [e] but back instead of front. The IPA transcription would be [ɤ]. Cf. Bloch and Trager (1942, 22), Trager (1964, 16). Abercrombie (1967, 161) suggests [ə] for the original IPA [ë] (cf. *JIPA* 5, 52). Catford (1977, 178) and Trager (1964, 16) use it also. *Comments:* The result of the change in the IPA's interpretation of the umlaut and its common use with a different sense in American practice is a rather confusing situation in which [ë] may denote a centralized front vowel (official IPA), a central vowel (*Principles*), or a back vowel (e.g. Bloch and Trager).

E with Polish Hook

IPA Usage: Not used; not to be confused with [e̜] (right-hook *e*). *American Usage:* Nasalized [e]. Boas et al. (1916, 8) recommend the use of a centered subscript rightward hook as a nasalization diacritic, and this is still used (instead of the IPA's tilde diacritic) by some authorities, e.g. Smalley (1963, 333). The diacritic is found indicating nasalization in Polish orthography, hence our name for it. *Other uses:* Used by some editors of Old English texts (e.g. Bright 1935 and Sweet 1882) to distinguish orthographic *e*'s (IPA [ɛ]) which resulted from umlaut. Does not occur in the original manuscripts. Cf. Moore and Knott (1955, 12).

Right-hook E

IPA Usage: Recommended in *Principles* (p. 14) for a vowel with the quality of [e] (i.e. Cardinal 2) with rhotacization (*r*-coloration). Approval of the right-hook diacritic (q.v.) was withdrawn in 1976 (*JIPA* 6, 3) in favor of a digraph such as [eɹ] or [eʲ]. *American Usage:* Not used. The rightward hook used by the IPA for indicating rhotacization should not be confused with the centered "Polish hook"; for example, [ą] is used in Polish orthography and Americanist transcription for nasalized vowels.

SCHWA

IPA USAGE

Mid central unrounded vowel.

AMERICAN USAGE

Same as IPA.

OTHER USES

Used by Jerzy Kuryłowicz, and by other Indo-Europeanists subsequently, to represent Saussure's "laryngeals". Kuryłowicz wrote $\langle \mathfrak{a}_1 \rangle$, $\langle \mathfrak{a}_2 \rangle$, etc., for distinct postulated laryngeals. See Polomé (1965) for a thorough discussion and references to the literature.

COMMENTS

Used for a range of distinguishable non-peripheral vowels for which other symbols could also be used; thus [ə] may represent in broad transcriptions a retracted and only slightly rounded [œ] in French, [ɐ] in word-final position in British English, [ɜ] in stressed positions in British English, [ɨ] in many American dialects, and so on.

There is a wide range of variation in the articulatory descriptions given to schwa by American phoneticians. Bloch and Trager (1942, 22) define it as mean-mid central. Pike (1947, 5) gives it as upper-mid central. Smalley (1963, 363) shows it as lower-mid central. Gleason (1955, 8) does not distinguish [ə] from [ʌ] and describes [ə] as mid central or back. On the distinction between [ə] and [ʌ], see the unintendedly confusing note by Cartier and Todaro (1983, 17).

Following in this tradition, Chomsky and Halle (1968, 176) do not include [ə] in their chart showing the feature composition of English segments, though they use the symbol [ə] throughout. This is because they write [ə] for a totally unstressed vowel and deliberately take no position on the question of its precise phonetic realization (59, n. 1;

245, n. 7). Hence they espouse no phonetic description corresponding to [ə], though they note (59, n. 1) that for many speakers it may be [ɨ]. Their feature system apparently does not allow for the representation of a distinction between IPA [ɨ], [ə], and [ʌ].

SOURCE

Roman alphabet lower-case *e,* turned (rotated 180°). The name *schwa* or *shva* (Hebrew *sh'wa*) comes from traditional Hebrew grammar (Prokosch 1939, 94).

RIGHT-HOOK SCHWA

IPA USAGE

Recommended in *Principles* (p. 14) (in the form [ɚ]) for a mid or upper-mid vowel with the quality of [ə] with rhotacization (*r*-coloration). Described as "another way of writing frictionless ɹ when used as a vowel." Approval of the general use of the right-hook diacritic (q.v.) was withdrawn in 1976 (*JIPA* 6, 3) in favor of a digraph such as [əɹ] or [əˀ], though this character in the form ⟨ɚ⟩ and the character ⟨ɝ⟩ for a similar sound were deemed useful enough to be retained.

AMERICAN USAGE

Same as IPA, if used.

COMMENTS

The rightward hook used by the IPA for indicating rhotacization should not be confused with the centered "Polish hook"; for example, [ą] is used in Polish orthography and Americanist transcription for a nasalized vowel, not a rhotacized one.

The IPA's decision to withdraw recognition from the rhotacization diacritic was prompted by an opinion of the secretary of the IPA, who said of the symbols for rhotacized vowels: "I think no one but Jones ever really liked these symbols, and even he was not enthusiastic" (*JIPA* 5, 57).

SOURCE

Schwa, with IPA's right-hook diacritic for rhotacization.

REVERSED E

IPA USAGE

Not officially sanctioned but suggested (*JIPA* 5, 52) for a half-close
(upper-mid) central unrounded vowel, midway between [e] and [ɤ].
Used by Abercrombie (1967, 161) and Catford (1977, 178) for a cardinal central unrounded vowel of the same height as Cardinal 2.

AMERICAN USAGE

Not generally used, though Kurath (1939, 123) and Trager (1964, 16)
list it with an interpretation that agrees with the unofficial IPA usage.

COMMENTS

This symbol is an ⟨e⟩ reversed left-to-right, i.e. the mirror image of
⟨e⟩. It should not be confused with the much more common symbol
⟨ə⟩ (schwa), which is an ⟨e⟩ that has been turned (i.e. rotated 180°).

SOURCE

Roman alphabet, lower-case ⟨e⟩, modified by lateral reversal.

SMALL CAPITAL E

AMERICAN USAGE

Not standard, but used by Bloch and Trager (1942, 22) for a front unrounded vowel at exactly the mid point ("mean-mid"), i.e. between Cardinal 2 and Cardinal 3. Used in this way in Crothers (1978, 137). The recommendations of Boas et al. (1916, 10) concerning the use of small capital letters would make [E] the transcription of voiceless [e].

SOURCE

Roman alphabet, small capital *e*. Note that the character is distinct from both ⟨ɛ⟩ and ⟨E⟩.

Small Capital E Umlaut

IPA Usage: Not used. *American Usage:* Not in use, but suggested by Bloch and Trager (1942, 22) for a "mean-mid" (i.e. mid) back unrounded vowel (i.e. between Cardinals 6 and 7 but unrounded). See also Trager (1964, 16), where alternative transcriptions [Ë] and [Δ] are suggested for this vowel. The corresponding IPA transcription would be [ɤ̞] or [ʌ̞].

Capital E

IPA Usage: Not used. *American Usage:* Boas et al. (1916, 10) recommend the use of small capitals to represent the voiceless versions of normally voiced sounds (either vowels or sonorants), and following this, Pike (1947, 5) and Smalley (1963, 392) both use a general convention of capital letters for voiceless vowels; thus the transcription [E] might be used for IPA [e̥]. *Other uses:* In Indo-Europeanist work, used for a non-*a*-coloring laryngeal (see Hamp 1965a, 123, n. 3), and in Chomsky and Halle (1968, chaps. 2–4) to represent informally the vocalic nucleus that is realized as [ɛ] when lax and [i:] when tense.

EPSILON

IPA USAGE

Cardinal vowel No. 3: lower-mid front unrounded.

AMERICAN USAGE

Same as IPA, when used.

OTHER USES

Al-Ani (1970, 29) uses ⟨ɛ⟩ for the voiced pharyngeal fricative (IPA [ʕ]), presumably for its visual similarity to the Arabic character ⟨ ع ⟩. Cf. the entry for *Turned 3*.

As a superscript, used by early Americanists (e.g. in the *Handbook of American Indian Languages*) to indicate a glottal stop. Thus the transcription [ᵋɑ´tcī'] by William Jones (1911, 742) corresponds to something like IPA [ˌʔatʃiːʲ].

Used by Chomsky and Halle (1968, 161, 176, 228n, 229, 245n) for a hypothetical mid front glide in English which causes certain phonological effects (e.g. the change of [t] to [s] in the alternation *resident/residence*, the latter having an underlying final /ɛ/) but is always removed by an elision rule in derivations so that it never surfaces phonetically.

SOURCE

Greek epsilon (in some fonts). The other way of printing epsilon, ⟨ϵ⟩, (which is common in mathematical texts as the set membership sign) is not generally used, though it may be found (cf. Sapir 1925, 43). The character occurred as a vowel symbol (with the value IPA [i]) in Isaac Pitman's 1845 Phonotypic alphabet (cf. Pitman and St. John 1969, p. 82).

Epsilon with Over-dot

IPA Usage: Not used. *American Usage:* Not in general use. Following the recommendations of Boas et al. (1916, 10), used by Bloch and Trager (1942, 22) for a lower-mid central unrounded vowel; cf. also Trager (1964, 16), who gives [ɜ] (*Reversed Epsilon,* q.v.) as an alternative. The corresponding *Principles*-type transcription would be [ë].

Right-hook Epsilon

IPA Usage: Recommended in *Principles* (p. 14) for a vowel with the quality of [ɛ] (i.e. Cardinal 3) with rhotacization (*r*-coloration). Approval of the right-hook diacritic (q.v.) was withdrawn in 1976 (*JIPA* 6, 3) in favor of a digraph such as [ɛɹ] or [ɛ']. *American Usage:* Not used. The rightward hook used by the IPA for indicating rhotacization should not be confused with the centered "Polish hook"; for example, [ą] is used in Polish orthography and Americanist transcription for a nasalized vowel.

Closed Epsilon

Occurs in Kurath (1939, 125) for IPA [œ], a rounded lower-mid front vowel. An invention for use in the linguistic atlas of New England, used chiefly to transcribe the vowel sound in the pronunciation of English *bird* in some dialects which do not have an *r*-colored vowel. A logical analogy: [ɛ]:[ɵ]::[ɜ]:[ɞ].

REVERSED EPSILON

IPA USAGE

Sanctioned in *Principles* (p. 7) as "another variety of a central vowel." Listed under "Other Symbols" below the 1979 revised chart (see Cartier and Todaro 1983, 84) as a "variety of ə." Used by Abercrombie (1967, 161) and Catford (1977, 178) to represent a central unrounded vowel of the same height as Cardinal 3.

AMERICAN USAGE

Seldom used, but Kurath (1939, 123) and Trager (1964, 22) use it for a lower-mid central unrounded vowel, as an alternative to [ɛ].

OTHER USES

Used as a typographical compromise for yogh (q.v., p. 178) in the transliterations of texts in Jones (1972, chap. 2) and in Trubetzkoy (1969, 73).

COMMENTS

Reversed epsilon was introduced primarily to represent the vowel of educated Southern British English ("received pronunciation" or RP, in the terminology of Daniel Jones [see Jones 1918]) in such words as *bird*. Jones did not use the symbol, writing [ə:] instead (see e.g. 1962, 88–91, and 1956, 47), but it does appear in Gimson (1962, 116–18, and later editions). Jones suggests in various places (see especially 1962, 64) that [ə:] is higher than [ə] in RP, suggesting that [ɜ:] should be taken as somewhat higher than mid. This disagrees with Trager, with Catford (1977, 178), and with Kurath and McDavid (1961, 1). However, Gimson (1962, 116) notes that a wide range of variants of the RP /ɜ/ phoneme are found, some lower than Cardinal 3 and some higher than Cardinal 2; he assigns /ə/ a very similar range (1962, 119) and questions the correctness of assuming distinct /ɜ/ and /ə/ phonemes (1962, 116). The assignment of the symbol ⟨ə⟩ to represent a

mid vowel, ⟨ ɘ ⟩ to represent an upper-mid vowel, and ⟨ɜ⟩ to represent
a lower-mid vowel (on which Trager and Catford have settled) should
be regarded as arbitrary, and not directly connected to Gimson's use of
⟨ɜ⟩ and ⟨ə⟩ in describing RP phonetics and phonemics.

SOURCE

Greek alphabet, lower-case epsilon, modified by left-right reversal.

RIGHT-HOOK
REVERSED EPSILON

Suggested (*JIPA* 5, 57) as useful enough to be retained for the rho-tacized (*r*-colored) version of [ɜ] when general approval of the right-hook rhotacization diacritic (q.v.) on vowels was withdrawn in favor of digraphs. The symbol is given in Cartier and Todaro's (1983, 11) English vowel chart, though not in their revised IPA chart (p. 84).

AMERICAN USAGE

Not in general use, but found, e.g., in Kenyon (1950).

COMMENTS

The IPA's decision to withdraw recognition from the general use of the rhotacization diacritic was prompted by an opinion of the secretary of the IPA, who said of the symbols for rhotacized vowels: "I think no one but Jones ever really liked these symbols, and even he was not enthusiastic" (*JIPA* 5, 57).

SOURCE

Greek alphabet lower-case epsilon, laterally reversed, with the IPA's right-hook diacritic for rhotacization.

CLOSED REVERSED EPSILON

Not officially sanctioned, but considered (*JIPA* 5, 52) for a half-open central rounded vowel, intermediate between [œ] and [ɔ], and used in just this way by Abercrombie (1967, 161) and Catford (1977, 178): for a central rounded vowel of the same height as Cardinal 3. Catford states that the sound is "only a little more central than the French vowel of *note*."

AMERICAN USAGE

Not generally used, though it occurs in Kurath (1939, 123) with a sense compatible with the usage of Abercrombie and Catford.

SOURCE

Invention; created apparently by closing the shape of a laterally-reversed Greek lower-case epsilon ⟨ε⟩.

LOWER-CASE F

IPA USAGE

IPA USAGE

Voiceless labiodental central fricative.

AMERICAN USAGE

Same as IPA.

COMMENTS

May be used for [Φ] in languages like Japanese which have [Φ] but no [f]. However, some languages, e.g. Ewe and Logba of the Kwa group in West Africa have a [Φ]-[f] contrast (see Ladefoged 1968, 25).

SOURCE

Roman alphabet, lower case.

Barred Dotless J
See page 84.

Script Lower-case F

Used in the International African Institute's orthography for African languages for a voiceless bilabial fricative, IPA [Φ]. Cf. *Practical Orthography for African Languages* and Tucker (1971). Also used in Westermann and Ward (1933; see pp. 77–79).

Small Capital F

Given by Kurath (1939, 140) for a sound "resembling *f* . . . but with less friction and usually shorter," the voiceless correspondent to script *v,* and therefore presumably a voiceless frictionless labiodental approximant.

LOWER-CASE G

Voiced velar (or advanced velar) stop.

AMERICAN USAGE

Voiced velar stop.

COMMENTS

Not always used for a phonetically voiced stop; in languages like Mandarin Chinese and Icelandic, it may be used in broad transcription or in orthography for an unaspirated voiceless stop that contrasts with an aspirated one.

A little-known IPA recommendation (*Principles,* 14) suggests using the symbol ⟨ɡ⟩ for advanced velar stops and the symbol ⟨g⟩ for ordinary velar stops where the two are distinguished. This does not seem to have struck phoneticians as a good idea, and the two variants of lower case *g* are generally regarded as interchangeable. Cf. Albright 1958, 59.

Something like this contrast (but with the symbols switched) is used by Wright (1910, 50) in his transcription of "Indogermanic." The symbols ⟨k⟩ and ⟨g⟩ are given as "palatal" stops and ⟨q⟩ and ⟨ɡ⟩ as "true velars."

SOURCE

Roman alphabet, lower case.

Barred G

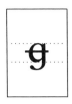

IPA Usage: Not used. *American Usage:* Not standard; but both Pike and Smalley suggest barred *g* to represent a voiced velar fricative (IPA [ɣ]). (N.B. Pike 1947 seems to have a typo, ⟨g⟩ for ⟨ǥ⟩, at several points in the chart on p. 7.) *Comments:* Barred stop symbols (with a superimposed hyphen or short dash through the body of the letter) are often used to represent those fricatives for which the IPA symbols are not used. The resultant symbols have the advantage of being easy to type on an unmodified typewriter.

Crossed G

IPA Usage: Not used. *American Usage:* Occasionally found for a voiced velar fricative (IPA [ɣ]). *Comments:* By a general convention, barred stop symbols (with a superimposed hyphen or short dash through the body of the letter) are often used to represent those fricatives for which the IPA symbols are not used. The resultant symbols have the advantage of being easy to type on an unmodified typewriter. The superimposed dash crosses the descender of ⟨g⟩ in (e.g.) Jespersen (1949, 22) and Meillet and Cohen (1952, xiii). Presumably this character was formed by analogy with *Crossed D* and *Crossed B* (q.v.).

HOOKTOP G

IPA USAGE

Hooktop *g* is not given in the *Principles* booklet, but it is suggested that voiced implosives be represented as "ɓ, ɗ, etc." Subsequently the symbol was officially adopted for a velar implosive (see the 1979 revised IPA chart: Cartier and Todaro 1983, 84).

AMERICAN USAGE

Same as IPA: glottalic ingressive (i.e. implosive) velar stop.

COMMENTS

The sound [ɠ] is rather rare, but Maddieson (1984, 217) cites Swahili, Maasai, Nyangi, Ik, Yulu, and Angas as languages that exemplify it.

SOURCE

Roman alphabet lower-case *g*, modified.

SMALL CAPITAL G

IPA USAGE

Voiced uvular stop.

AMERICAN USAGE

Same as IPA, if used; recommended by Trager (1964, 22) for a voiced postvelar (i.e. uvular) stop.

COMMENTS

Voiced correspondent of [q]. Encountered in Eskimo, and (allophonically) in Teherani Persian (Farsi) (*Principles,* 35). Contrasts with both [q] and [qʰ] in Burushaski according to Catford (1977, 160).

Smalley regards uvular stops like [ɢ] as "backed velars," and transcribes [ɢ] as [g̱].

SOURCE

Roman alphabet, small capital font.

Capital G

IPA Usage: Not used.   *American Usage:* May be found as a typographical substitute for the small capital ⟨ɢ⟩ (voiced uvular stop); see e.g. Pike 1947.   *Other uses:* Used for the morphophoneme proposed by Hamp (1951) to represent the trigger of Gemination, an initial consonant mutation in Old Irish.

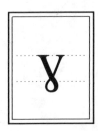

GAMMA

IPA USAGE

Used in *Principles* (p. 10) for a voiced velar fricative or frictionless approximant. The approximant value was withdrawn in favor of the transcription [ɰ] in the 1979 revision.

AMERICAN USAGE

Same as IPA.

COMMENTS

Must be carefully distinguished from the IPA's ⟨ɤ⟩, "baby gamma" (which Smalley 1963, 363, unfortunately calls "gamma"). Gamma descends below the line and denotes a fricative consonant as heard in Modern Greek γαμμα 'gamma', *g* in German *sagen* 'to say', and Spanish *hago* 'I make'. Baby gamma represents a mid back unrounded vowel.

Doke (1926a, 1926b) uses gamma for a voiced dental click in languages like Zulu and Ɓhũː Bushman that do not have a voiced velar fricative, but this usage is not found in recent work.

The characters ⟨ɣ⟩ ("front-tailed gamma") and ⟨γ⟩ ("back-tailed gamma") were proposed by Trager for a voiced, prevelar slit spirant (i.e. voiced fronted velar fricative) and a voiced postvelar slit spirant (i.e. voiced uvular fricative, IPA [ʁ]) respectively. These suggestions never caught on.

SOURCE

Greek alphabet, lower case. The other form of gamma, ⟨γ⟩, is not the standard IPA character, but may occasionally be found. Cf. Sapir (1925, 43).

BABY GAMMA

IPA USAGE

Cardinal vowel No. 15: upper-mid back unrounded. The secondary cardinal vowel corresponding to Cardinal 7.

AMERICAN USAGE

Same as IPA, if used.

COMMENTS

Must be carefully distinguished from ⟨ɣ⟩ (gamma). Smalley (1963, 363) actually calls this vowel symbol "gamma," using ⟨ǥ⟩ "barred *g*" for the fricative IPA [ɣ]. This is a potential source of serious confusion, as is the occurrence of occasional printers' errors on this point; for example, the [ɤ] on p. 72 of Bleek (1926) is an error for [ɣ].

SOURCE

The character was used as a vowel symbol (with the value IPA [au]) in Isaac Pitman's 1845 Phonotypic alphabet (cf. Pitman and St. John 1969, 82). The name "baby gamma" was coined by Kenneth Pike, according to Trager (1964, 15).

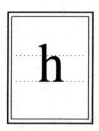

LOWER-CASE H

IPA USAGE

Voiceless glottal central fricative or approximant.

AMERICAN USAGE

Same as IPA.

OTHER USES

Indo-Europeanists write ⟨h⟩ for a voiceless velar fricative in some cases, e.g. in Germanic languages, where an earlier velar fricative has become glottal in modern dialects (cf. Old vs. Modern English).

COMMENTS

A segment broadly represented as [h] may have a very wide range of phonetic variation; e.g., between [ɸ], [ç], [ḁ], [e̥], and [o̥] in Japanese.

SOURCE

Roman alphabet, lower case.

Superscript H

The approved (*JIPA* 6, 2) alternative to the reversed apostrophe as a diacritic used after a stop symbol to represent aspiration. More common, in fact, than the reversed apostrophe.

Under-dot H

IPA Usage: Not used. (In principle, should represent a "closer" variety of the glottal fricative [h], but this has no clear phonetic meaning.)   *American Usage:* Occasionally found representing a voiceless pharyngeal fricative, IPA [ħ], particularly in transliterations of Arabic. Recommended by Boas et al. (1916, 14) for such a sound, in this instance apparently conflicting with their general interpretation of the under-dot as a retraction diacritic.

H-V Ligature

IPA Usage: Not used. *Principles* (p. 14) recommends [hw] or [ʍ] for voiceless [w].   *American Usage:* Not generally used. The symbol is recommended by Boas et al. (1916, 12) for a voiceless [w], following the use for Gothic.   *Other uses:* Used as the roman alphabet transliteration of the Gothic letter ⟨Θ⟩, described as "either a labialized **h** or else a voiceless **w**" (cf. Wright 1910, 11).   *Comments:* A ligature composed of *h* and *v*, created to emphasize the fact that the sound patterns as a single consonantal unit in the Gothic sound system.

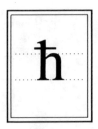

CROSSED H

IPA USAGE

Voiceless pharyngeal central fricative.

AMERICAN USAGE

Same as IPA, if used.

COMMENTS

It was recommended to the IPA (see *Principles,* p. 19) that ⟨ħ⟩ be re-placed by ⟨ ⟩, which is visually reminiscent of Arabic ⟨ ⟩ (*ḥa*), but the suggestion has not found its way into practice.

SOURCE

Roman alphabet lower-case *h,* with superimposed crossbar.

HOOKTOP H

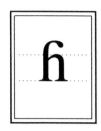

IPA USAGE

Voiced (or murmured) glottal fricative or approximant.

AMERICAN USAGE

Same as IPA, if used.

COMMENTS

The right-facing hooked top indicates an implosive in [ɓ], [ɗ], [ɠ], but not here.

SOURCE

Roman alphabet lower-case *h,* modified.

Superscript Hooktop H

IPA Usage: Indicates voiced glottal fricative release, or indication of similarity to a voiced glottal fricative. *American Usage:* Used by Pike (1947, 7) with voiced stop symbols as a digraph for murmured or voiced aspirated stops; cf. also Ladefoged 1982, 258.

Hooktop H with Rightward Tail

Used by Prokosch (1939, 50) for a voiceless fortis velar fricative in his discussion of Grimm's Law. He contrasts [f þ ꜧ] (voiceless fortis) with [φ θ χ] (voiceless lenis). The symbol seems to be hooktop *h* with a rightward turning tail. It occurs in Prokosch only in italic font, and so it could simply be a form of an italic hooktop *h* which has an exaggerated right leg.

HOOKTOP HENG

IPA USAGE

Recommended (*Principles*, 14) for a "combination of **x** and ʃ (one variety of Swedish *tj*, *kj*, etc.)."

AMERICAN USAGE

Not used.

COMMENTS

The IPA description appears to mean that *tj* and *kj* in the Swedish orthography may correspond to a voiceless fricative articulated with simultaneous velar and palato-alveolar friction.

The symbol is rarely seen, and would need a note of explanation if used.

SOURCE

A visual compromise between ⟨h⟩ and ⟨ʃ⟩?

Heng

This symbol was suggested (only half seriously) by Yuen-Ren Chao (1934, 52) as the symbol for a putative phoneme uniting English /h/ (which only occurs at the beginnings of syllables) and /ŋ/ (which only occurs at the ends of syllables). This symbol does not occur in phonetic transcriptions because it is not associated with any fixed set of phonetic properties—which is exactly the point of Chao's discussion. Included here for typographical continuity in the family of *h*-based characters (and because calling it *heng* allowed us to devise a name for the otherwise unnameable ⟨ɧ⟩).

TURNED H

IPA USAGE

Voiced rounded palatal approximant. (Rounded counterpart of [j]; the semivowel corresponding to [y].)

AMERICAN USAGE

Not used.

COMMENTS

As heard in French *lui* [lɥi], not the same as *Louis* [lwi].

SOURCE

Roman alphabet lower-case *h,* turned (rotated 180°). Visually suggestive of ⟨y⟩, the IPA symbol for the corresponding vowel.

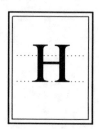

CAPITAL H

IPA USAGE

Not used.

AMERICAN USAGE

Sometimes used (e.g. by Smalley 1963, 181) to represent the putative phoneme in the Trager-Smith analysis of English that has [h] as its realization in prevocalic position and is realized as [ə] in postvocalic position. Not found in phonetic transcriptions; purely a phonological abstraction.

OTHER USES

Used by Holger Pedersen, and by other Indo-Europeanists subsequently, to represent Saussure's "laryngeals." Pedersen used ⟨H₁⟩ and ⟨H₂⟩ to represent specific distinct phonemes of Proto-Indo-European. ⟨H⟩ is used to refer to the class including both of them, or, in a theory propounded by L. L. Hammerich, to represent a conjectured unique PIE laryngeal. See Polomé (1965) for a thorough discussion and references to the literature.

SOURCE

Roman alphabet, upper case.

η *Eta*
See page 104.

LOWER-CASE I

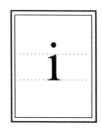

IPA USAGE

Cardinal vowel No. 1: high front unrounded.

AMERICAN USAGE

Same as IPA.

COMMENTS

Not the same as ⟨ɩ⟩ or ⟨ɪ⟩.

SOURCE

Roman alphabet, lower case. ⟨i⟩ represents [i] in most languages that use the letter (with the exception of English, where it represents [i] in *machine*, but [aɪ] in *shine*, [ɪ] in *shin*, and so on).

I Umlaut

IPA Usage: According to *Principles* (p. 16), a high central un-rounded vowel, an alternative to [ɨ], though the current interpretation of the umlaut diacritic (q.v.) makes it a central*ized* high front un-rounded vowel between [i] and [ɨ]. *American Usage:* According to the widely followed recommendation of Boas et al. (1916, 9) on the use of the umlaut (q.v.) with vowel symbols, [ï] would represent a high back unrounded vowel, i.e. a vowel with all of the properties of [i] but back instead of front. The IPA transcription would be [ɯ]. Cf. Pike (1947, 5) and Trager (1964, 16). *Comments:* The result of the change in the IPA's interpretation of the umlaut and its common use with a different sense in American practice is a rather confusing situation in which [ï] may denote a centralized front vowel (official IPA), a central vowel (*Principles*), or a back vowel (e.g. Bloch and Trager). *Source:* The character is a Roman alphabet lower-case *i*, with umlaut diacritic. When the umlaut is added to a dotted letter, it is customary for it to replace the dot, though sometimes in typewritten work one may encounter ⟨ï⟩.

Undotted I

IPA Usage: Not sanctioned. *American Usage:* Not used, except perhaps sometimes as a typographical substitute for ⟨ɪ⟩ or ⟨ɩ⟩. *Comments:* Occurs in Turkish orthography, representing IPA [ɯ], and thus should ideally not be used for IPA [ɩ] if ⟨ɩ⟩ or ⟨ɪ⟩ is available. The character is a lower-case *i* with its dot removed. It was introduced into the Turkish alphabet in the 1928 orthography reform that replaced the earlier Arabic-based writing system.

BARRED I

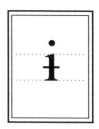

IPA USAGE

High central unrounded vowel, between Cardinal 1 and Cardinal 8.

AMERICAN USAGE

Often same as IPA, but there is some variation: Pike (1947, 5) agrees with the IPA, but Smalley (1963, 284) lists the symbol as denoting an unrounded central vowel that is "lower-high," i.e. semi-high like [ɪ] and [ʊ]; and some sources collapse central high vowels with back: Gleason (1955, 8) cites [ɨ] as either central or back, and Halle and Clements (1983, 29) state that [ɨ] represents the same sound as [ɯ], which is definitely not the case under the IPA's definition of the latter. They give no symbols for any back unrounded vowels other than [ɑ], which is quite peculiar.

COMMENTS

Barred *i* has often been used by American scholars in the transcription of English, for words with a schwa that is pronounced somewhat higher than the mid line; for example, the word *just* has been transcribed [ǰɨst].

SOURCE

Roman alphabet lower-case *i*, modified with superimposed hyphen.

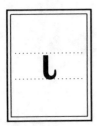

IOTA

IPA USAGE

Semi-high front (or retracted front) unrounded vowel, between Cardinal 1 and Cardinal 2.

AMERICAN USAGE

Same as IPA if used, though ⟨ɪ⟩ is common.

COMMENTS

Sometimes [ɪ] is regarded as differing from [i] in tenseness rather than height, [i] being tense and [ɪ] lax.

The symbol ⟨ɪ⟩ might be regarded as interchangeable with ⟨ɪ⟩, and with ⟨ɪ⟩ or ⟨I⟩ if typographical considerations render it necessary.

SOURCE

Greek alphabet correspondent to Roman alphabet *i*.

SMALL CAPITAL I

IPA USAGE

Sanctioned as a typographical substitute for ⟨ɪ⟩: semi-high front (or retracted front) unrounded vowel, between Cardinal 1 and Cardinal 2.

AMERICAN USAGE

Semi-high front unrounded vowel, between Cardinal 1 and Cardinal 2. Sometimes [ɪ] is regarded as differing from [i] in tenseness rather than height, [i] being tense and [ɪ] lax.

OTHER USES

The recommendations of Boas et al. (1916, 10) on the use of small capital letters would make [ɪ] the transcription of a voiceless [i].

COMMENTS

The symbol ⟨ɪ⟩ might be regarded as interchangeable with ⟨ɪ⟩, and with ⟨ı⟩ or ⟨I⟩ if typographical considerations render it necessary.

Small Capital I Umlaut

IPA Usage: Not used. *American Usage:* According to the widely followed recommendations of Boas et al. (1916, 9) on the use of the umlaut with vowel symbols, where [ɪ] is used to represent IPA [ɪ], [ï] would represent a semi-high back unrounded vowel (between [ï] and [ë]), i.e. a vowel with all of the properties of [ɪ] but back instead of front. Cf. Bloch and Trager (1964, 22). The IPA transcription for such a vowel would be [ɯ̈] or [ɯ̞] or [ɰ̈]. Pike (1947, 5) suggests the very similar symbol ⟨ɨ̮⟩ for this sound. Trager (1964, 16) proposes ⟨ъ⟩ as an alternative.

Barred Small Capital I

IPA Usage: Not used. *American Usage:* Not common, but given by Bloch and Trager (1942, 22) for a lower-high central unrounded vowel, a logical extension of the character [ɪ] (lower-high front unrounded) by use of the superimposed hyphen on analogy with [ɨ]. Used by Halle and Mohanan (1985, 91) for a high back unrounded vowel, IPA [ɯ].

Capital I

IPA Usage: Not used. *American Usage:* Boas et al. (1916, 10) recommend the use of small capitals to represent the voiceless versions of normally voiced sounds (either vowels or sonorants). Pike and Smalley both suggest the use of capital letters for voiceless vowels; thus the transcription [I] might be used for IPA and standard American [i̥]. *Other uses:* ⟨I⟩ is also sometimes found as a typographical substitute for iota, being available, unlike any special symbol, on an unmodified typewriter. Thus it may represent a semi-high front unrounded voiced vowel [ɪ]. In Chomsky and Halle (1968, chaps. 2–4), *I* is used to represent informally the vocalic nucleus that is realized as [ɪ] when lax and [ay] (in their transcription) when tense.

LOWER-CASE J

IPA USAGE

Voiced palatal central approximant or fricative.

AMERICAN USAGE

No standard use. The following uses have been found in American linguistics literature:

Sometimes used with the same value as the IPA recommends, though [y] should be regarded as standard American for the voiced palatal approximant.

Sometimes written for IPA [dʒ] (voiced palato-alveolar affricate), especially in broad transcription of English, though [ǰ] should be regarded as standard for the voiced palato-alveolar affricate.

Boas (1911, 23): voiced dental fricative, IPA [ð].

Boas et al. (1916, 5): voiced palato-alveolar fricative, IPA [ʒ]. (This usage was supplanted by the later recommendations of Herzog et al. that [ž] be used for [ʒ].)

Sapir (1925, 23): voiced palato-alveolar fricative, IPA [ʒ].

Smalley (1963, 275): voiced alveopalatal stop, IPA [ɟ+].

OTHER USES

Standardly used by Indologists and Dravidianists for voiced palatal or palato-alveolar stops or affricates in languages such as Sanskrit, Hindi, and Tamil. See e.g. Whitney (1889, 2).

COMMENTS

In a rare case of sanctioned ambiguity, *Principles* (p. 13) recommends use of the same symbol for a voiced fricative and a frictionless approximant at the palatal place of articulation "since the two varieties have not been found to exist as separate phonemes in any language." Thus it appears in two positions in the IPA's consonant chart.

However, the reasoning expressed in *Principles* is now known not to be phonetically justified. Hoffmann (1963) reports that Bura and Margi have a contrast between palatal fricatives and approximants. Ladefoged (1968, 28; 1971, 59–60) confirms the observation for Margi. John Wells in *JIPA* 5 (1975, 54) cites other languages with such a contrast ("Gaelic, some varieties of German and Spanish, and perhaps Modern Greek").

JIPA 6 (1976, 2–3) subsequently reports agreement in the Council of the IPA that the ambiguity should be resolved. Nonetheless, resolution of the ambiguity between the approximant and fricative values for IPA [j] was deferred in 1976 because the council split on whether to retain [j] as a palatal approximant or to use [y] instead. The 1979 chart leaves the symbol ambiguous.

The disagreement between the IPA and other systems on the use of ⟨y⟩ and ⟨j⟩ is an ongoing problem. *Principles* notes that the "World Orthography" described in *Practical Orthography of African Languages* differs from the IPA *only* in "that *j* and *y* are taken to have their English consonantal values."

The letter ⟨j⟩ represents a variety of consonants in different orthographies: [ʒ] in French, [x] in Spanish, [dʒ] in English, and, agreeing with its IPA value, [j] in German and the Scandinavian languages (note the Norwegian loanword *fjord* in English).

SOURCE

Roman alphabet, lower case; as used for various Germanic languages. The phonological unit corresponding to ⟨j⟩ is sometimes referred to as "jod" by Germanicists and other linguists.

Superscript J

IPA Usage: Indicates a coloration of [j] quality, i.e. modification in the direction of high, front, unrounded (palatal approximant) articulation. Thus [tʲ] would be equivalent to [t̡]: a palatalized [t]. *American Usage:* Generally not used, a superscript ⟨y⟩ being used instead.

Hooktop J

IPA Usage: Not used. *American Usage:* Proposed by Smalley (1963, 378) for an "alveopalatal" implosive, but this seems to be his term for palatal, for he uses it in all cases where other systems would use "palatal." *Other uses:* The sound in question is reported in Sindhi (Ladefoged 1971, 26), and in Kadugli, Swahili, Maasai, Nyangi, Ik, Yulu, and Angas (Maddieson 1984, 217).

Barred J

IPA Usage: Not used. *American Usage:* Not standard. Proposed by Smalley (1963) for a voiced flat (i.e. not grooved) "alveopalatal" (palato-alveolar) fricative, and listed by Hyman (1975, 241) as a voiced palatal stop, i.e. IPA [ɟ]. The symbol is not in general use. Smalley's use of barred *j* is probably supposed to be equivalent to IPA [ ]. His use is consistent with a general convention that assigns barred stop symbols (with a superimposed hyphen or short dash through the body of the letter) to represent those fricatives for which the IPA symbols are not used. The resultant symbols have the advantage of being easy to type on an unmodified typewriter. Hyman's use seems to be merely a typographical compromise.

Curly-tail J

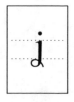

IPA Usage: Not officially sanctioned, but cited by the secretary of the IPA (*JIPA* 5, 55) as in use for a voiced palatal fricative, resolving the ambiguity of the official [j]. *American Usage:* Not used.

Small Capital J

IPA Usage: Not used. *American Usage:* Not used. *Other uses:* Used by Catford (1977, 120) for a "voiced dorso-palatal fricative." *Comments:* Catford uses this symbol without remark, though it is not standard. However, since it is known that the IPA system needs revision to incorporate a distinction between voiced palatal central approximant and voiced palatal fricative (see entry for ⟨j⟩), Catford's implicit suggestion is a useful one.

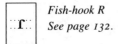

Fish-hook R
See page 132.

WEDGE J

IPA USAGE

Not used.

AMERICAN USAGE

Voiced palato-alveolar affricate with central fricative release (IPA [dʒ]).

COMMENTS

The recommendations of Herzog et al. (1934, 631) which formalized the use of the wedge diacritic in American transcription used [ǯ] as the transcription for IPA [dʒ]. The regular analogic pattern of their recommendations was interrupted by the replacement of [ǯ] by [ǰ], presumably as a typographical compromise. As an example, Hoijer (1945, 8) uses a transcription which is otherwise consistent with previous recommendations except in the use of ⟨ǰ⟩ for ⟨ǯ⟩. Cf. also Bloomfield (1933, 129), who uses ⟨ǰ⟩ for IPA [dʒ].

SOURCE

Roman alphabet lower-case *j*, with the *haček* ('little hook') or wedge used for certain palato-alveolar consonants in the Czech orthography.

BARRED DOTLESS J

IPA USAGE
Voiced palatal stop.

AMERICAN USAGE
Not generally used.

COMMENTS
As represented by *gy* in a Hungarian word like *Magyar* 'Hungarian'.

SOURCE
Typographically, a turned lower-case *f*, but better thought of as a variant of ⟨j⟩, since in English words like *job* a ⟨j⟩ represents a palato-alveolar affricate [dʒ] that is at least somewhat similar to IPA [ɟ], though not identical.

Hooktop Barred Dotless J

IPA Usage: Not explicitly sanctioned, but constructed in a way obviously in accord with IPA practice to suggest a palatal implosive. *American Usage:* Not standardly used. *Other uses:* The sound represented by this symbol is rather rare, and the IPA provides no representation for it at all, even in the 1979 revised chart, but Ladefoged (1971, 26) uses it, and gives Sindhi examples of the sound, and Maddieson (1984, 217) cites Kadugli, Swahili, Maasai, Nyangi, Ik, Yulu, and Angas as languages exemplifying it.

LOWER-CASE K

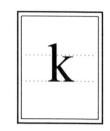

IPA USAGE
Voiceless velar stop.

AMERICAN USAGE
Same as IPA.

COMMENTS

Note [kʰ] for aspirated variant, [k'] for ejective (glottalic egressive) velar stop, [kʲ] for palatalized variant, etc.

Wright (1910, 51) gives [k] as a voiceless "palatal" stop in contrast to [q], a "true velar." What is considered the dividing line between *palatal* and *velar* sounds has apparently changed over time. Cf. also Boas et al. (1916). Presumably the denotations are the same; only the descriptive terminology has changed.

SOURCE

Roman alphabet, lower case.

Crossed K

Used in Meillet and Cohen 1952 (xiii) for a voiceless "velar" fricative. A logical extension of the convention for using barred forms of stop symbols for the homorganic fricatives.

Hooktop K

Represents a voiceless velar ejective (IPA [k']) in the orthographies of some African languages (e.g. Hausa). The character is constructed with the rightward-swept hook at top which is used by the IPA to create characters for implosive consonants, though it does not represent an implosive.

Turned K

IPA Usage: Originally recommended (*Principles,* 14) for a velaric ingressive velar stop (i.e. a velar click); but it seems clear that this is not in fact articulatorily possible. The primary consonantal obstruction must be further forward than the velum in order for the velaric airstream mechanism to be usable, since a dorso-velar closure is maintained while the body of the tongue is lowered to create suction. We know of no reports of velar clicks in any language, and the symbol for them no longer appears in the 1979 revision of the IPA chart (Cartier and Todaro 1971, 84). *Other uses:* Used in some early work by Dorsey on Ponca (Siouan) to represent unaspirated [k], so that ⟨k⟩ could be used for the aspirated [kʰ] (see Boas and Swanton 1911, 881). *Source:* Roman alphabet lower-case ⟨k⟩, turned (rotated 180°).

LOWER-CASE L

IPA USAGE

Voiced alveolar lateral approximant.

AMERICAN USAGE

Same as IPA.

COMMENTS

Takes various diacritics to show phonetic modifications: [l̥] (voiceless), [l̩] (syllabic), [ɫ] (velarized, as in English "dark" postvocalic /l/), [lʲ] (palatalized), [ḷ] (retroflex, in American usage), etc.

Kurath (1939, 138) gives [l̪] as a distinctly "clear *l*" with no velarization at all.

SOURCE

Roman alphabet, lower case.

L with Tilde

IPA Usage: Velarized ("dark") voiced alveolar lateral approximant, as in English postvocalic laterals, e.g. in *all*. *American Usage:* Same as IPA. Sometimes found as a substitute for barred *l* (IPA [ɫ]), i.e. a voiceless alveolar lateral fricative. This substitution can lead to ambiguity and is best avoided.

BARRED L

IPA USAGE

Not used.

AMERICAN USAGE

Voiceless alveolar lateral fricative (IPA [ɬ]). The character is used by Boas et al. (1916, 7) as an alternative to small capital *l* for the voiceless version of [l].

COMMENTS

As represented by ⟨ll⟩ in Welsh and in Greenlandic Eskimo.

The character is sometimes used with the bar slanted, i.e. ⟨ł⟩, a character used in the Polish orthography for a sound like IPA [w]; see e.g. Chomsky and Halle (1968, 317). Tilde *l* is also sometimes substituted. The original form (cf. Boas et al. 1916, 7), however, is an *l* with a superimposed horizontal dash or hyphen, and it seems best to use it to avoid confusion with these other characters.

SOURCE

Roman alphabet lower-case *l*, with superimposed hyphen.

BELTED L

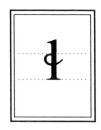

IPA USAGE

Voiceless alveolar lateral fricative.

AMERICAN USAGE

Same as IPA, if used. Barred *l* (q.v.) is sometimes used instead.

COMMENTS

As represented by ⟨ll⟩ in Welsh and in Greenlandic Eskimo.

SOURCE

Roman alphabet lower-case ⟨l⟩, with superimposed curved belt.

L WITH RIGHT TAIL

IPA USAGE

Voiced post-alveolar (retroflex) lateral approximant.

AMERICAN USAGE

Not used. The usual equivalent is [ļ], using the under-dot diacritic of Boas et al. (1916, 10) to indicate retracted articulation.

COMMENTS

The retroflexion diacritic used by the IPA in [ʂ] and [ʐ] is echoed by the rightward-swept elongation of the rightmost vertical stroke of a character in the IPA's special symbols for other retroflex consonants: [ɳ], [ʈ], [ɖ], and [ɽ]. In the interests of terminological consistency, we recognize in this family resemblance an IPA retroflexion indicator, which we call "right tail" (q.v.).

SOURCE

Roman alphabet lower-case *l*, modified with the IPA diacritic for retroflexion.

L-YOGH LIGATURE

IPA USAGE

Voiced alveolar lateral fricative.

AMERICAN USAGE

Same as IPA, if used.

COMMENTS

As represented by ⟨dhl⟩ in Zulu orthography. Found in a number of African languages, e.g. Bura and Margi (Chadic; Ladefoged 1968, 29) as well as Zulu and Xhosa (Southern Bantu; see *Principles* pp. 50–51 for Xhosa).

SOURCE

This symbol is in origin a ligature of ⟨l⟩ and ⟨ʒ⟩, though this is not entirely evident from the versions of it that have been produced for some IPA fonts, including the one used for printing *Principles* itself.

CAPITAL L

IPA USAGE

Not used.

AMERICAN USAGE

Not standard, but may be found for a voiceless alveolar lateral.

OTHER USES

Among Celticists, used to indicate a nonmutated *l* in (e.g.) Carmody 1945. Used for the morphophoneme proposed by Hamp 1951 to represent the triggers of Lenition, an initial consonant mutation in Celtic languages. Cf. also McCloskey 1979, 8–9.

COMMENTS

The standard transcription for a voiceless [l] would be [l̥] or [ɬ]. Following the recommendation of Boas et al. (1916, 10) that small capital letters be used for the voiceless versions of normally voiced sounds, Pike (1947, 7) and Smalley (1963, 217) both suggest [L] for IPA [l̥].

SOURCE

Roman alphabet, upper case.

Small Capital L

IPA Usage: Not used. *American Usage:* Not in use, but proposed by Bloch and Trager (1942, 16) and by Trager (1964, 22) for a voiced "dorsal" (Bloch and Trager) or "medio-velar" (Trager) lateral. Wells (1982, xvii; cf. vol. 3, 6.5.9) may be following this proposal in using small capital *l* for a velar lateral, more specifically "a lip-rounded vocoid with close back tongue position and unilateral velar closure" (vol. 3, p. 551), citing Caffee (1940) for the original description of the sound in Southern U.S. English. May be typed as a full-size capital, ⟨L⟩, which is in fact what Trager (1964) does, though he calls the symbol "small-cap *l*" (p. 21), following Bloch and Trager. *Other uses:* Boas et al. (1916, 10) recommend that small capital letters be used for the voiceless versions of normally voiced sounds and hence [ʟ] could be found for a voiceless lateral approximant (IPA [l̥]).

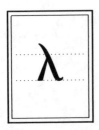

LAMBDA

IPA USAGE

Not used.

AMERICAN USAGE

Voiced alveolar laterally released affricate: IPA [dl].

OTHER USES

Recommended by Boas et al. (1916, 13) for a "dorsal" (i.e. palatal) lateral approximant, presumably IPA [ʎ].

SOURCE

Greek alphabet correspondent of ⟨l⟩. Used for [dl] in early work on Eskimo by Jenness, and recommended for standard Americanist use by Herzog et al. (1934, 631). Note that we take IPA [ʎ] to be a turned *y*, q.v., rather than a laterally reversed lambda.

Turned Y
See page 171.

Crossed Lambda

IPA Usage: Not used.   *American Usage:* Voiceless alveolar laterally released affricate (IPA [tl̥]). The character is a Greek lambda with a superimposed short slash. Invented on analogy with barred *l* as the voiceless correspondent of [λ] by Herzog et al. (1934, 631).

LOWER-CASE M

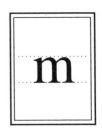

IPA USAGE

Voiced bilabial nasal.

AMERICAN USAGE

Same as IPA.

COMMENTS

Takes various diacritics to show phonetic modifications: [m̥] (voiceless), [m̩] (syllabic), etc.

SOURCE

Roman alphabet, lower case.

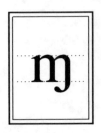

M WITH LEFTWARD TAIL AT RIGHT

IPA USAGE

Voiced labiodental nasal.

AMERICAN USAGE

Not used.

COMMENTS

Very rare. Represents a sound that is never found phonologically distinct from [m].

In [g] and [ŋ] the left-facing downward tail on the rightmost edge connotes velar articulation, but not here.

Catford (1977, 192) uses this symbol for a palatalized [m], but this appears to be a typographer's error for ⟨mʲ⟩, i.e. ⟨m⟩ with the IPA's palatalization diacritic, left hook (q.v.).

SOURCE

Roman alphabet lower-case ⟨m⟩, modified.

TURNED M

IPA USAGE

Cardinal vowel No. 16: high back unrounded. The secondary cardinal vowel corresponding to Cardinal 8.

AMERICAN USAGE

Standardly the same as IPA, if used; but various alternatives, including [ï] and [ɨ], are found.

COMMENTS

As represented by ⟨ı⟩ in Turkish orthography. The Japanese vowel transliterated as ⟨u⟩ is similar to this, having virtually no rounding.

Halle and Clements (1983, 29) assert that "ɯ = ɨ," but this is definitely not the case under the IPA's definitions, or in standard American. It can only be regarded as a defensible claim under the analysis of vowels in the Chomsky and Halle tradition, where all vowels are treated phonologically as either front or back ([−back] or [+back]).

SOURCE

Roman alphabet lower-case ⟨m⟩, turned (rotated 180°). Visually suggestive of two *u*'s, or of *w*, and thus hinting at high back tongue position. The character was used as a vowel symbol (with the value IPA [u]) in Isaac Pitman's 1845 Phonotypic alphabet (cf. Pitman and St. John 1969, p. 82).

TURNED M WITH LONG RIGHT LEG

IPA USAGE

Approved in 1976 (*JIPA* 6, 3) for a voiced velar median (central) approximant, the glide corresponding to [ɯ]. The symbol resolves the ambiguity of [ɣ], which has only its fricative value now.

AMERICAN USAGE

Not in use, but recommended by Trager (1964, 16) for a back unrounded semivowel.

COMMENTS

Despite the differing terminology above, the 1979 IPA system and Trager's 1964 system are in agreement. The sound in question can be described either as a semivowel (glide) with the properties 'high', 'back', and 'unrounded', or as a central (nonlateral) approximant consonant with velar place of articulation. The sound can be regarded as an unrounded [w].

This symbol has not seen much use. Ladefoged (1968, 26) suggests that Bini has such a sound, but transcribes it as [ɣ⊤]. Likewise, Maddieson lists five languages (Kanakuru, Aranda, Adzera, Wiyot, and Cofan) claimed to have the segment in question, but transcribes it [y̬].

SOURCE

Invention, possibly by Trager, involving the addition of a tail to the IPA's ⟨ɯ⟩, to suggest on the one hand ⟨ɯ⟩ and on the other hand the IPA's ⟨ɥ⟩. Trager calls the symbol "double-turned *h*."

Inverted W
See page 164.

CAPITAL M

IPA USAGE

Not used.

AMERICAN USAGE

Not standard, but following the recommendation of Boas et al. (1916, 10) that small capital letters be used for the voiceless versions of normally voiced sounds, Pike (1947, 7) and Smalley (1963, 192) both suggest [M] for IPA [m̥].

COMMENTS

Not frequently found.

SOURCE

Roman alphabet, upper case.

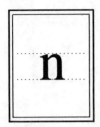

LOWER-CASE N

IPA USAGE

Voiced dental or alveolar nasal. [n̪] indicates definitely dental; [n] may be either if no contrast is to be indicated, but will be taken to be alveolar as a default assumption.

AMERICAN USAGE

Same as IPA.

COMMENTS

Takes various diacritics to show phonetic modifications: [n̥] (voiceless), [n̩] (syllabic), [n̪] (dental), etc. Note that some diacritics indicate more radical differences in denotation: [ñ] is a common transcription for an alveopalatal or palatal nasal stop, [ń] is used in the orthography of Polish for a palatal nasal stop, IPA [ɲ].

SOURCE

Roman alphabet, lower case.

N Acute

Suggested by Trager (1964, 22) for a prepalatal (i.e. fronted palatal) nasal. Following the orthography of some Slavic languages (e.g. Polish), [ń] might be found as a transcription for the palatal nasal, IPA [ɲ].

Front-bar N

Proposed by Trager (1964, 22) for a dental nasal, IPA [n̪] or American [y̰].

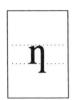

N with Long Right Leg

IPA Usage: Proposed in *Principles* (p. 14) for representing a syllabic alveolar nasal, particularly as in Japanese, or as a digraph for nasal vowels (p. 16). IPA approval was withdrawn in 1976 (*JIPA* 6, 3) because the symbol is purely phonological, being realized in Japanese by a number of different sounds. The symbol ⟨n̩⟩ is normally used for a syllabic [n].

TILDE N

IPA USAGE

Not used.

AMERICAN USAGE

Voiced palato-alveolar or palatal nasal.

COMMENTS

Gleason, Pike, and Smalley use ⟨ñ⟩ for a palato-alveolar nasal ("alveopalatal" in their terms), using ⟨ṇ̃⟩ (Gleason) or ⟨ṇ⟩ (Smalley) for a true palatal one.

Used throughout Boas 1910 and recommended by Boas et al. (1916) as a typographical compromise for the voiced velar nasal. The eng (⟨ŋ⟩) is the standard symbol.

SOURCE

Roman alphabet lower-case *n,* with tilde (as in Spanish orthography).

N WITH LEFTWARD HOOK AT LEFT

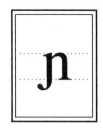

IPA USAGE

Voiced palatal nasal.

AMERICAN USAGE

Same as IPA, if used, but various alternatives are commonly employed: ⟨ŋ̡⟩ (Gleason 1955), ⟨ŋ̢⟩ (Smalley 1963), and very commonly ⟨ñ⟩.

COMMENTS

Illustrated by the sound represented *gn* in French and Italian, *ñ* in Spanish, etc.

SOURCE

Roman alphabet lower-case ⟨n⟩, modified with the leftward-facing tail or hook used by the IPA for symbols denoting palatal or palatalized sounds.

IPA USAGE

Voiced velar nasal.

AMERICAN USAGE

Same as IPA.

COMMENTS

Illustrated by the sound represented *ng* in English words such as *thing* and *n* in words such as *think*.

SOURCE

Roman alphabet lower-case *n*, modified with a tail reminiscent of the tail of a ⟨g⟩. The symbol is known as either "eng" or "angma" and occurred in this form with this value in Isaac Pitman's 1845 Phonotypic alphabet (cf. Pitman and St. John 1969, 82). Albright (1958, 11) suggests that it goes back to Holder in 1669. Brugman (1904, 1) uses a similar symbol.

Eta

The Greek alphabet character eta is used by some printers as a substitute for ⟨ŋ⟩, especially in italic fonts. The printer of *American Anthropologist* unfortunately did this to Herzog et al. (1934, 630–31). We assume that their recommendation is that eng and not eta is to be used for the velar nasal. It represents a vowel pronounced [i] in Modern Greek.

N WITH RIGHT TAIL

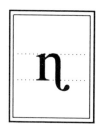

IPA USAGE

Voiced retroflex (i.e. apico-postalveolar) nasal.

AMERICAN USAGE

Not used.

COMMENTS

Illustrated by the sound represented ⟨ण⟩ in Hindi, Marathi, etc. American and Indological practice uses [ṇ] for this sound.

The retroflexion diacritic used by the IPA in [ʂ] and [ʐ] is echoed by the rightward-swept elongation of the rightmost vertical stroke of a character in the IPA's special symbols for other retroflex consonants: [ʈ], [ɖ], [ɭ], and [ɽ]. In the interests of terminological consistency, we recognize in this family resemblance an IPA retroflexion indicator, which we call "right tail" (q.v.).

SOURCE

Roman alphabet *n*, modified with the IPA diacritic for retroflexion.

SMALL CAPITAL N

IPA USAGE

Voiced uvular nasal.

AMERICAN USAGE

Same as IPA, if used, but usually not found, [ŋ] often being used instead.

Boas et al. (1916, 10) recommend that small capital letters be used for the voiceless versions of normally voiced sounds and hence [N] could be found for a voiceless alveolar nasal (IPA [n̥]).

COMMENTS

Found in Eskimo. Also found according to *Principles* (p. 36) in Persian (Farsi), as an allophone of /n/ before /q/.

Following the terminology of Boas et al. (1916, 4), Smalley (1963) does not recognize uvular consonants as such, but uses the term "backed velar" instead. For the backed velar nasal, Smalley uses ⟨ŋ⟩.

SOURCE

Roman alphabet, small capital font.

Capital N

IPA Usage: Not used. (Not to be confused with ⟨n⟩.) *American Usage:* Not standard. Following the recommendation of Boas et al. (1916, 10) that small capital letters be used for the voiceless versions of normally voiced sounds, Pike (1947, 7) and Smalley (1963, 192) both suggest [N] for IPA [n̥]. *Other uses:* Also found in lexical and phonological representations representing a nasal "archiphoneme," i.e. to denote a segment that is a nasal stop unspecified for place of articulation (and realized phonetically in various ways depending on the properties of adjacent segments). Thus the lexical representation of English *think* might be given as /θiNk/. Among Celticists, used to indicate a nonmutated [n] (cf. Carmody 1945). Used for the morphophoneme proposed by Hamp 1951 to represent the triggers of the initial consonant mutation Nasalization in Celtic languages. Cf. also McCloskey 1979, 8–9.

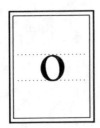

LOWER-CASE O

IPA USAGE

Cardinal vowel No. 7: upper-mid back rounded.

AMERICAN USAGE

Same as IPA.

COMMENTS

As in French *beau,* IPA [bo]. The English vowel in *toe* is generally diphthongal, varying between [ow] and [əѡ], but standardly represented [oѡ] in broad transcription.

SOURCE

Roman alphabet, lower case.

O with Over-dot

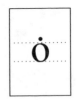

IPA Usage: Not used. *American Usage:* Not in general use. Following the recommendations of Boas et al. (1916, 10) for the use of an over-dot as a diacritic for central vowels, used by Bloch and Trager (1942, 22) for a "higher-mid" rounded central vowel. Trager (1964, 16) suggests [ɵ] as an alternative. The equivalent IPA transcription is [ɵ], [ɵ̞], or [ɵ˲].

O Umlaut

IPA Usage: According to *Principles* (p. 16), a rounded mid central vowel (between [ø] and [o]); a rounded schwa, equivalent to [ɵ]. The current interpretation of the umlaut diacritic (q.v.) makes it a central*ized* rounded mid back vowel, between [o] and [ɵ]. *American Usage:* According to the widely followed recommendation of Boas et al. (1916, 9) on the use of the umlaut (q.v.) with vowel symbols, [ö] would be a rounded higher-mid front vowel, i.e. a vowel with all of the properties of [o] but front instead of back. The IPA transcription would be [ø]. Cf. Bloch and Trager (1942, 22), Trager (1964, 16). *Other uses:* The symbol is used in the orthographies for a number of Germanic languages with essentially its *Principles* value. *Comments:* The result of the change in the IPA's interpretation of the umlaut and its common use with a different sense in American practice is a rather confusing situation in which [ö] may denote a centralized back vowel (official IPA), a central vowel (*Principles*), or a front vowel (e.g. Bloch and Trager).

O with Polish Hook

IPA Usage: Not used; not to be confused with right-hook *o*. *American Usage:* Boas et al. (1916, 8) recommend the use of a centered subscript rightward hook as a nasalization diacritic. Sometimes used instead of the IPA's tilde diacritic, as by Smalley (1963, 333). *Other uses:* Used by some editors of Old English texts (e.g. Bright 1935 and Sweet 1882) to distinguish orthographic *o*'s (IPA [ɔ]) which developed from [a]. Does not occur in the original manuscripts (Moore and Knott 1955, 33). Used for Old Norse to represent IPA [ɔ], which developed from [a] by *u*-mutation (Prokosch 1939, 110). *Source:* The symbol is roman alphabet lower-case *o* with the hook used in Polish orthography to mark nasal vowels.

Capital O

IPA Usage: Not used. *American Usage:* Boas et al. (1916, 10) recommend the use of small capitals to represent the voiceless versions of normally voiced sounds (either vowels or sonorants). Pike and Smalley both suggest the use of capital letters for voiceless vowels; thus the transcription [O] might be used for IPA [o̥]. *Other uses:* In Chomsky and Halle (1968, chaps. 2–4), *O* is used to represent informally the vocalic nucleus that is realized as [ɔ] when lax and [ow] when tense. Used in Crothers (1978, 137) for a mid back rounded vowel (Bloch and Trager's "mean-mid" vowel [ɒ]).

Female Sign

Not in general use, but proposed by Trager (1964, 22) for a voiced pharyngeal stop. The extent to which this invention is unlikely to be called upon can be gauged from the fact that, according to Catford (1977, 22–23), two muscles that allow for constriction of the pharynx are actually missing in many members of the human species—in about 80% of Japanese people, for example. Certainly pharyngeal stop consonants appear not to be definitely attested in any language.

This symbol is familiar from nonlinguistic disciplines; in astronomy it denotes the planet Venus, and in biology it is used to indicate an organism of the female gender.

Uncrossed Female Sign

Not in use, but proposed by Trager (1964, 22) for a voiceless pharyngeal stop. See the previous entry on the nonoccurrence of this symbol and the sound it represents.

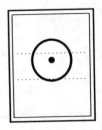

BULL'S EYE

IPA USAGE

Velaric ingressive bilabial stop (i.e. bilabial click). Not mentioned in *Principles*, but approved by the IPA in 1976 (*JIPA* 6, 2).

AMERICAN USAGE

Same as IPA.

COMMENTS

A bilabial velaric ingressive stop is essentially a kiss. It is reported as a consonant in a number of Southern Bushman languages (though Doke 1926b, 126, denied the existence of such a click, defining clicks entirely in terms of lingual articulation, and asserting that the Bushman sound in question is a labiovelar plosive).

SOURCE

Attributed by Doke (1926b, 126) to W. H. I. Bleek (no reference cited). Introduced into the IPA inventory in the 1979 revision.

BARRED O

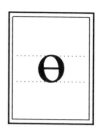

IPA USAGE

Rounded mid central vowel, i.e. rounded schwa; "intermediate between ø and o."

AMERICAN USAGE

Not used. Following the recommendation of Boas et al. (1916, 10) on the use of the over-dot diacritic, [ȯ] would be a central round vowel intermediate between [o] and [ö]. Gleason (1955, 2), Pike (1947, 5), and Halle and Clements (1983, 31) use ⟨ö⟩ for IPA [ø], and offer no symbol for a rounded mid central vowel.

COMMENTS

As in Swedish *dum,* according to *Principles* (p. 9) which also sanctions transcribing [ɵ] as [ö] (though see the entry for ⟨ö⟩).

SOURCE

Roman alphabet lower-case *o,* modified by superimposed hyphen. The character occurs as a vowel symbol (with the value IPA [ɔ]) in Isaac Pitman's 1845 Phonotypic alphabet (cf. Pitman and St. John 1969, 82).

Theta
See page 151.

SLASHED O

Cardinal vowel No. 10: upper-mid front rounded. The secondary cardinal vowel corresponding to Cardinal 2.

AMERICAN USAGE

Same as IPA, if used. But Gleason (1955, 2), Pike (1947, 5), and Halle and Clements (1983, 31), for example, use ⟨ö⟩ instead.

COMMENTS

Illustrated by French *peu* and German *schön*.

This symbol should be carefully distinguished from Greek phi and slashed zero, though not all typesetters have appreciated this: in Quirk and Wrenn (1957, 122), [ø] is set as ⟨φ⟩, and in Ingram (1976, xvi), [φ] is set as [ø]; these occurrences should be regarded as printing and editing errors.

SOURCE

Roman alphabet lower-case *o,* with superimposed oblique stroke; as used in Danish orthography.

O-E LIGATURE

IPA USAGE

Cardinal vowel No. 11: lower-mid front rounded. The secondary cardinal vowel corresponding to Cardinal 3.

AMERICAN USAGE

Same as IPA, if used (as it is e.g. by Smalley). But Pike, Halle and Clements, and others used ⟨ɔ̈⟩ instead.

COMMENTS

Illustrated by the vowel sounds in French *œuf* (short [œ]) and *veuve* (long [œ:]), and by German *zwölf*.

SOURCE

Ligature of *o* and *e,* as used in French orthography.

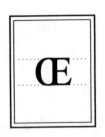

SMALL CAPITAL O-E LIGATURE

IPA USAGE

Approved in 1976 for Cardinal vowel No. 12: low front rounded. The secondary cardinal vowel corresponding to Cardinal 4.

AMERICAN USAGE

Not in use, but proposed by Trager (1964, 16) for a mid front rounded vowel. The transcription in the Bloch and Trager system would be [ö].

COMMENTS

The IPA initially provided no symbol for a low front rounded vowel, "since this sound has not as yet been found to occur in any language as a phoneme separate from œ" (*Principles*, 6), but the 1979 revision added this symbol.

SOURCE

Ligature of small capitals *o* and *e*. *JIPA* 6 (1976, 54) attributes the symbol to the text accompanying Daniel Jones's 1956 recording of the cardinal vowels.

OPEN O

Cardinal vowel No. 6: lower-mid back rounded.

AMERICAN USAGE

Same as IPA, following the recommendations of Boas et al. (1916, 2). Occasionally used (e.g. Pike [1947, 5]) as a low (or upper-low) back rounded vowel, an alternative to IPA [ɒ].

COMMENTS

Illustrated by the vowel sound of the Scottish English pronunciation of *hot*, German *Sonne*, and (to a fair approximation) represented by *o* before *r* in French and most varieties of English (French *porte, fort;* English *corn*); cf. also British "RP" *caught.*

SOURCE

Roman alphabet lower-case *o*, modified. Typographically, lower-case ⟨c⟩ turned (rotated 180°). The character appears in this form and with this value in Henry Sweet's (1877) *A Handbook of Phonetics.*

Open O with Over-dot

IPA Usage: Not used. *American Usage:* Not standard. Following the recommendations of Boas et al. (1916, 10) on the use of the over-dot diacritic, used for a lower-mid central rounded vowel by Bloch and Trager (1942, 22). See also Trager (1964, 16). Trager suggests [x] as an alternative. The IPA transcription for a lower-mid central rounded vowel is [ɵ̞], [ɵ̞], or [ɵ⊤].

Open O Umlaut

IPA Usage: According to *Principles* (p. 16), a lower-mid rounded central vowel, between Cardinals 6 and 3, similar to a rounded [ɐ], though the current interpretation of the umlaut diacritic (q.v.) makes it a central*ized* lower-mid rounded back vowel, between [ɔ] and [ɵ⊤]. *American Usage:* According to the widely followed recommendation of Boas et al. (1916, 9) on the use of the umlaut (q.v.) with vowel symbols, [ɔ̈] would represent a rounded lower-mid or low front vowel, i.e. a vowel with all of the properties of [ɔ] but front instead of back. The IPA transcription would be [œ]. Cf. Bloch and Trager (1942, 22) where it is given as an alternative to [œ], Trager (1964, 16), Halle and Clements (1983, 31). Pike (1947, 5), who uses [ɔ] as a "close" (i.e. upper-) low back vowel correspondingly uses [ɔ̈] as a close low front vowel, IPA [œ]. *Comments:* The result of the change in the IPA's interpretation of the umlaut and its common use with a different sense in American practice is a rather confusing situation in which [ɔ̈] may denote a centralized back vowel (official IPA), a central vowel (*Principles*), or a front vowel (e.g. Trager).

Barred Open O

IPA Usage: Not used. *American Usage:* Not in use, but proposed by Trager (1964, 16) for a lower-mid central rounded vowel, as an alternative to the [ɔ] of Bloch and Trager (1942, 22). The IPA equivalent is [ɵ̞], [ɵ̞], or [ɵᴛ]. The character is open *o* with superimposed hyphen (as in other symbols for central vowels, e.g. ⟨ɨ⟩, ⟨ʉ⟩, ⟨ɵ⟩).

Right-hook Open O

IPA Usage: Recommended in *Principles* (p. 14) for a vowel with the quality of [ɔ] (i.e. Cardinal 6, lower-mid back rounded) with rhotacization (*r*-coloration). Approval of the right-hook diacritic (q.v.) was withdrawn in 1976 (*JIPA* 6, 3) in favor of a digraph such as [ɔɹ] or [ɔ']. *American Usage:* Not used. The rightward hook used by the IPA for indicating rhotacization should not be confused with the centered "Polish hook"; for example, [ą] is used in Polish orthography and Americanist (e.g. Smalley 1963, 333) transcription for nasalized vowels.

Open O-E Ligature

IPA Usage: Not used. *American Usage:* Suggested by Trager (1964, 16), departing from Bloch and Trager (1942, 22), for a lower-mid front rounded vowel. The Bloch and Trager symbol for a low front rounded vowel is ⟨ö⟩ (1942, 22), and Trager (1964, 16) suggests this or ⟨ɒ⟩. The symbol was adopted by Chomsky and Halle (1968, 191–92) to represent the underlying low front rounded vowel that they postulate for English. Under Chomsky and Halle's analysis, the abstract segment represented by this symbol undergoes several rules shifting vowel quality and adding glides, and emerges phonetically as the diphthong written [ɔy] by Chomsky and Halle (IPA [ɔɪ]). *Comments:* The IPA's *Principles* provides no symbol for a low front rounded vowel, "since this sound has not as yet been found to occur in any language as a phoneme separate from *œ*" (p. 6), but a small capital *o-e* ligature, ⟨Œ⟩, was approved for such a vowel in 1976 (*JIPA* 6, 2).

LOWER-CASE OMEGA

IPA USAGE

Not used.

AMERICAN USAGE

Not in general use, but used by Bloch and Trager (1942, 16) following
Boas et al. (1916, 10) for a higher-low back rounded vowel, between
IPA [ɔ] and [ɒ].

OTHER USES

Used by Wells (1982, xvii) for an unrounded [ʊ]: semi-high back
unrounded.

COMMENTS

Not to be confused with ⟨w⟩, ⟨ɯ⟩, or ⟨ω⟩. The IPA transcription corresponding to Bloch and Trager's [ω] is [ɔ̞], [ɔ̞], [ɔ̞ꞇ], [ɒ], [ɒ̞],
or [ɒ˖].

SOURCE

Greek alphabet, lower case.

Lower-case Omega with Over-dot

IPA Usage: Not used. *American Usage:* Not in general use. Following the recommendation of Boas et al. (1916, 10) for the use of the
over-dot diacritic (q.v.) for central vowels, used by Bloch and Trager

(1942, 22) for a higher-low central rounded vowel—the same height as IPA [æ], but central and rounded. Trager (1964, 16) suggests [ɷ] as an alternative. A suitable *Principles*-type transcription for Bloch and Trager's [ɷ] is [œ̨] (or [œ̈], or [œ̨̈]).

Lower-case Omega Umlaut

IPA Usage: Not used. *American Usage:* According to the widely followed recommendation of Boas et al. (1916, 9) on the use of the umlaut (q.v.) with vowel symbols, if [ω] represents a higher-low back rounded vowel, [ω̈] would represent a rounded higher-low front vowel, i.e. a vowel with all of the properties of [ω] but front instead of back. Cf. Bloch and Trager (1942, 22). Not in general use. Not to be confused with ⟨w⟩, ⟨ɯ⟩ or ⟨ɷ⟩. A suitable IPA transcription corresponding to Block and Trager's [ω̈] is [œ] (or [œ̨], or [œτ]). Trager (1964, 16) suggests [ɶ] as an alternative. Note that front rounded vowels lower than IPA [œ] are essentially unattested.

Inverted Lower-case Omega

IPA Usage: Not used. *American Usage:* Not in use, but proposed by Trager (1964, 16) for a higher-low central rounded vowel—the same height as IPA [æ] but central and rounded. An alternative to the [ɷ] of Bloch and Trager (1942, 22). A Trager suggestion that never caught on. A suitable equivalent *Principles*-type transcription is [œ̨̈] (or [œ̨̈], or [œ̈τ]).

Small Capital Omega

IPA Usage: Not used. *American Usage:* Not widely used, but recommended by Bloch and Trager (1942, 22; see also Trager 1964, 16) for a mid back rounded vowel ("mean-mid" in Bloch and Trager's terms, i.e. between the height of Cardinals 6 and 7, IPA [ɔ] and [o]). The IPA transcription for such a vowel would be [o̞], [ɔ̝], [oт], [ɔ⊥], [o̞], or [ɔ̞]. *Other uses:* A large capital omega is used by some Indo-Europeanists for an *o*-coloring laryngeal (see e.g. Hamp 1965a, 123, n. 3).

Small Capital Omega with Over-dot

IPA Usage: Not used. *American Usage:* Not in use, but following the recommendations of Boas et al. (1916, 10) on the use of the over-dot (q.v.) as a diacritic for central vowels, used by Bloch and Trager (1942, 22; see also Trager 1964, 16) for a mid central rounded vowel ("mean-mid" in Bloch and Trager's terms, i.e. between the height of Cardinals 2 and 3, IPA [e] and [ɛ]). Trager suggests [ɵ] as an alternative. Neither symbol has gained currency. The IPA equivalent transcription is [ɵ̞].

Small Capital Omega Umlaut

IPA Usage: Not used. *American Usage:* Not in general use. According to the widely followed recommendation of Boas et al. (1916, 9) on the use of the umlaut (q.v.) with vowel symbols, where [Ω] is Bloch and Trager's "mean-mid" back rounded vowel, [Ω̈] would represent a rounded mean-mid front vowel, i.e. a vowel with all of the properties of [Ω] but front instead of back, between the height of Cardinals 2 and 3, IPA [e] and [ɛ]. Cf. Bloch and Trager (1942, 22) and Trager (1964, 16). Trager suggests [œ] (q.v.) as an alternative, but note that this character has since been adopted by the IPA for a *low* front rounded vowel, i.e. Cardinal 12 (*JIPA* 6, 2).

Barred Small Capital Omega

IPA Usage: Not used. *American Usage:* Not in use, but an extension of the superimposed hyphen as a diacritic for central vowel symbols (cf. [ɨ], [ʉ], and [ɵ]) proposed by Trager (1964, 16) for a mid central rounded vowel, as an alternative to the [Ω̇] of Bloch and Trager (1942, 22). A Trager suggestion that never caught on. The IPA equivalent is [ɵ].

CLOSED OMEGA

IPA USAGE

Semi-high back rounded vowel, between Cardinal 7 and Cardinal 8.

AMERICAN USAGE

Not used; [ʊ] is generally used instead.

COMMENTS

Illustrated by the vowel sound in words such as *put* and *look* in Southern British English.

SOURCE

The character was used as a vowel symbol (with the value IPA [o]) in Isaac Pitman's 1845 Phonotypic alphabet (cf. Pitman and St. John 1969, 82), where it is the lower-case print form of a closed script *w*.

 Closed Reversed Epsilon
See page 55.

LOWER-CASE P

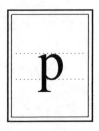

IPA USAGE

Voiceless bilabial stop.

AMERICAN USAGE

Same as IPA.

COMMENTS

Note related sounds such as [pʰ] (aspirated), [p'] (ejective), [pʷ] (labialized), etc. Smalley (1963, 48), following a general convention for barring consonant symbols to derive fricative symbols, uses [ₚ]for a voiceless bilabial fricative, IPA [Φ].

[p̌] is used in Trubetzkoy (1968, 69) for a voiceless labiodental affricate, IPA [pf].

SOURCE

Roman alphabet, lower case.

Barred P

IPA Usage: Not used.   *American Usage:* Not standard, but used by both Pike and Smalley (1947, 1963) for a voiceless bilabial fricative (IPA [Φ]).   *Comments:* Barred stop symbols (with a superimposed hyphen or short dash through the body of the letter) are often used to represent those fricatives for which the IPA symbols are not used. The resultant symbols have the advantage of being easy to type on an unmodified typewriter. The form ⟨p⟩ is used by Meillet and Cohen (1952, xiii).

Capital P

Used for the morphophoneme proposed by Hamp 1951 to represent the triggers of Provection, an initial consonant mutation in Welsh and Breton.

Wynn

A runic symbol adopted for the Old English orthography which represented the voiced rounded labiovelar approximant (IPA [w]). Wynn is not a phonetic transcription symbol and most editors of Old English texts substitute ⟨w⟩ for it to forestall confusion of it with ⟨p⟩ or thorn ⟨þ⟩ (q.v.). The eighth of the runes of the Germanic fuþark. Cf. Quirk and Wrenn (1957, 7–8).

THORN

IPA USAGE

Not sanctioned, but see e.g. the transcription scheme set out by Jespersen (1962, 235), which is broadly IPA throughout except that it has [þ] for [θ].

AMERICAN USAGE

Not used in modern work.

OTHER USES

Used by historical scholars, especially Germanicists, as a phonetic symbol for a voiceless interdental fricative, IPA [θ]; see e.g. Brugmann (1904), Prokosch (1939), Jespersen (1949, 1962), and many others.

COMMENTS

The symbols ⟨þ⟩ and ⟨ð⟩ were used indifferently in Late Old English manuscripts to represent the interdental fricative phoneme, which was voiced between two voiced sounds and voiceless elsewhere. Cf. Quirk and Wrenn (1957, 6–7). The character was borrowed into Scandinavian orthographies and is used in transliterations of other early Germanic languages; see e.g. Brugmann (1904, 1), Wright (1910, 4).

SOURCE

The third of the runes of the Germanic futhark. There is typographical variation, suggested below. Common attempts to produce the character on a typewriter are to overstrike *b* and *p*, or to position a lower-case *o* beside a slash (⟨/⟩). Thorn was sometimes written like a ⟨y⟩, the source of ⟨yᵉ⟩, and later *ye*, for English *the*.

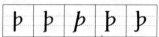

PHI

IPA USAGE

IPA USAGE

Voiceless bilabial fricative.

AMERICAN USAGE

Same as IPA.

COMMENTS

The *f* of the usual romanization of Japanese represents [ɸ]. In some languages, e.g. Ewe (West Africa), [ɸ] and [f] contrast.

The typographical variant symbol ⟨φ⟩ and the upper case correspondent ⟨Φ⟩ are not used in transcription; the ⟨Φ⟩ found in Hughes and Trudgill (1979, ix) is an error. The symbol ⟨ɸ⟩ should also be carefully distinguished from ⟨ø⟩ and ⟨Ø⟩; Ingram (1976, xvi) has [ø] as an error for ⟨ɸ⟩, and Quirk and Wrenn (1957, 122) have the converse error, using a variety of phi where [ø] is intended.

SOURCE

Greek alphabet, lower case.

LOWER-CASE Q

IPA USAGE

Voiceless uvular stop.

AMERICAN USAGE

Same as IPA when used.

OTHER USES

Wright (1910, 5) uses [q] to represent the labialized voiceless "velar" (see below) stop in Gothic.

In the Pinyin transliteration of Mandarin Chinese, ⟨q⟩ does not represent anything like a uvular stop, but instead stands for an alveolopalatal affricate, IPA [tɕ].

COMMENTS

Pike and Smalley regard uvular stops like [q] as "backed velars," and transcribe [q] as [k]. Wright (1910, 51) gives [q] as a "velar" stop and [k] as a "palatal" stop in his transcription for "Indogermanic." Boas et al. (1916, 4) consider [k] to be "palatal" and [q] to be "retracted palatal." What is considered the dividing line between *palatal* and *velar* sounds has apparently changed over time. Presumably the denotations are the same; only the descriptive terminology is different.

SOURCE

Roman alphabet lower-case *q*, traditionally used for transcribing the voiceless uvular stop of Arabic.

LOWER-CASE R

IPA USAGE

Voiced apico-alveolar trill.

AMERICAN USAGE

Usually same as IPA, but will often be used for other varieties of
"*r*-sound," especially the English frictionless continuant, IPA [ɹ].

COMMENTS

Being the easiest symbol to type or write, out of the many that are
used for "*r*-sounds," this symbol will often be used in broad transcription to represent sounds other than the alveolar trill that it officially represents in IPA terms. The alveolar trill may be heard in Scottish English, or in most varieties of Spanish (the *rr* of *perro* 'dog').

The symbol ⟨r⟩ is combined with a number of diacritics to indicate
varieties of *r*-sound in American usage. The tilde, the wedge, and the
underdot are particularly frequent. The (superscript) tilde often marks
a trilled articulation (Pike 1947, 7; Smalley 1963, 456–57); the
wedge may mark the articulation as flapped (Pike 1947, 7; Smalley
1963, 456–57) or fricative (Maddieson 1984, 240); the underdot
generally marks the articulation as retracted, which may mean retroflex (Pike 1947, 7; Maddieson 1984, 241) or uvular (Pike 1947, 7;
Smalley 1963, 457).

SOURCE

Roman alphabet, lower case.

FISH-HOOK R

IPA USAGE

Voiced alveolar flap.

AMERICAN USAGE

Same as IPA, if used, but various alternatives are found. These include [d̆] (Smalley 1963, 246), [ř] (Gleason 1955, 7; Halle and Clements 1983, 29, but see p. 11), [D] (Chomsky 1964, 90).

COMMENTS

As in Spanish *pero* 'but': a single apical tap.

SOURCE

Roman alphabet lower-case *r*, modified by removal of the serif at top left.

R WITH LONG LEG

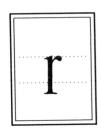

IPA USAGE

Voiced strident apico-alveolar fricative trill.

AMERICAN USAGE

Not used; ⟨ř⟩ will generally be used instead.

COMMENTS

This extremely rare sound is found in Czech, where it is denoted by ř.

SOURCE

Roman alphabet lower-case *r*, modified by lengthening the leg.

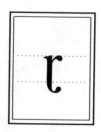

R WITH RIGHT TAIL

IPA USAGE

IPA USAGE

Voiced apico-postalveolar (i.e. retroflex) flap.

AMERICAN USAGE

Same as IPA, if used. [ɽ] may be used instead.

OTHER USES

Used in some work on African languages for a voiced alveolar flap, distinct from /l/ and /r/ in, e.g., Kreish (Gbaya). Also found in Indic languages such as Hindi/Urdu, Panjabi, and Bengali (see *Principles*, 36–37).

COMMENTS

The retroflexion diacritic used by the IPA in [ʂ] and [ʐ] is echoed by the rightward-swept elongation of the rightmost vertical stroke of a character in the IPA's special symbols for other retroflex consonants: [ɭ], [ɳ], [ʈ], and [ɖ]. In the interest of terminological consistency, we recognize in this family resemblance an IPA retroflexion indicator, which we call "right-tail" (q.v.).

SOURCE

Roman alphabet lower-case *r*, with the IPA diacritic for retroflexion.

TURNED R

IPA USAGE
Voiced alveolar frictionless continuant.

AMERICAN USAGE
Same as IPA, if used.

COMMENTS
The *r*-sound of many British and American dialects of English, also found in a variety of other languages (Maddieson 1984, 244).

   Essentially a nonsyllabic retroflex (i.e. rhotacized) central unrounded vowel. *Principles* (p. 14) refers to [ɚ] as "another way of writing frictionless ɹ when used as a vowel."

SOURCE
Roman alphabet lower-case *r*, turned (rotated 180°).

TURNED R WITH RIGHT TAIL

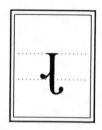

IPA USAGE

Voiced (median) retroflex approximant. Not given in *Principles*, but it appears in the 1979 chart (Cartier and Todaro 1983, 84).

AMERICAN USAGE

Not used.

COMMENTS

Often the *r*-sound of American English approximates a retroflex frictionless continuant. The sound is also encountered in many Australian languages and elsewhere (Maddieson 1984, 245).

The retroflexion diacritic used by the IPA in [ʂ] and [ʐ] is echoed by the rightward swept elongation of the rightmost vertical stroke of a character in the IPA's special symbols for other retroflex consonants: [ɭ], [ɳ], [ʈ], and [ɖ]. In the interest of terminological consistency, we recognize in this family resemblance an IPA retroflexion indicator, which we call "right-tail" (q.v.).

SOURCE

Turned *r*, the IPA's symbol for the voiced alveolar approximant, with the IPA diacritic for retroflexion.

TURNED
LONG-LEGGED R

Given in *Principles* (p. 14) for a "sound intermediate between d and l but distinct from l̥"; a voiced alveolar lateral flap.

AMERICAN USAGE

Not in general use, though the symbol may be known from Ladefoged (1971). It was used in the sense described above by Kurath (1939, 138).

COMMENTS

The symbol was invented by Daniel Jones to represent a sound found in Tswana, which he describes as "sounding between l and d" (Jones and Laver 1973, 193; see also Jones 1957, xv). It has often been used by others; see e.g. Doke (1926a, 142), and Ladefoged (1971, 52). The sound contrasts with IPA [ɾ], which *Principles* (p. 10) describes as "flapped" but Ladefoged calls a tap and Jones a "single flap." Ladefoged (1971, 51–52) says that "sounds having the characteristic gesture involved in making a flap may have in addition a distinctly lateral quality; when the articulation is formed there is contact only in the center of the mouth, so that momentarily there is a position similar to that of an l."

The sound is attested in Tswana according to Jones; in Ču: Bushman according to Doke; and in Haya and Chaga according to Ladefoged. It seems also to be a common variant of the /r/ sound of Japanese, though we have not seen this symbol used in the transcription of Japanese.

SOURCE

Apparently invented by Daniel Jones. The symbol is visually reminiscent of both ⟨l⟩ and ⟨r⟩.

SMALL CAPITAL R

IPA USAGE

Voiced uvular trill, as in (one variety of) the Parisian French *r*-sound.

AMERICAN USAGE

Not generally used. Pike (1947, 7) and Smalley (1963, 246) use [r̃] for the trilled uvular *r*.

OTHER USES

Boas et al. (1916, 10) recommend that small capital letters be used for the voiceless versions of normally voiced sounds and hence [ʀ] could be found for IPA [ʀ̥].

COMMENTS

Reserved for an actual trill; ⟨ʁ⟩ is used for the voiced uvular fricative.

SOURCE

Roman alphabet, small capital font.

Capital R

IPA Usage: Not used. (Not to be confused with ⟨ʀ⟩.) *American Usage:* Following the recommendation of Boas et al. (1916, 10) that small capital letters be used for the voiceless versions of normally voiced sounds, Pike and Smalley both suggest [R] for voiceless *r*-sounds like IPA [r̥], [ɹ̥], or [ʀ̥]. *Other uses:* Used to represent an unmutated *r* in Celtic languages in Carmody 1945.

INVERTED SMALL CAPITAL R

IPA USAGE

Voiced uvular fricative or frictionless approximant, as in some varieties of the French *r*-sound.

AMERICAN USAGE

Same as IPA, if used, but alternatives such as [ɣ] are found.

Note that Pike and Smalley do not recognize uvular obstruents as such, calling them "back[ed] velars," and using [ɡ̇] for the "backed velar" fricative.

COMMENTS

Reserved for a fricative or approximant; [ʀ] is used for the voiced uvular trill.

SOURCE

Roman alphabet small capital *r,* vertically inverted.

LOWER-CASE S

IPA USAGE

Voiceless alveolar central fricative.

AMERICAN USAGE

Same as IPA.

COMMENTS

Note [s̪] for dental variant, [s'] for ejective variant, etc. Note that some diacritics indicate a more radical change of denotation: [š] is the American transcription for a voiced alveopalatal fricative, IPA [ʃ], and [ś] is used in the Polish orthography and some comparative studies for a voiced laminal palatal fricative, IPA [c] (*Principles,* 12).

SOURCE

Roman alphabet, lower case.

Capital S

Used for the morphophoneme proposed by Hamp 1951 to represent the triggers of Spirantization, an initial consonant mutation in Welsh and Breton.

S WEDGE

IPA USAGE

Not used.

AMERICAN USAGE

Generally used in place of IPA's [ʃ] for a voiceless palato-alveolar central laminal fricative.

COMMENTS

The recommendation of Herzog et al. (1934, 631) on the use of the wedge in characters for palatoalveolar consonants required the substitution of [š] for the earlier use of [c], which came to be used for a voiceless alveolar affricate. This recommendation regarding [š] has been universally followed.

Used by Brugmann (1904, 1) with this value.

SOURCE

Roman alphabet lower-case *s*, with wedge diacritic, as used in the Czech orthography. The diacritic is called the *haček* ('little hook') in Czech and called "wedge" by many American linguists.

S WITH RIGHT TAIL

IPA USAGE

Voiceless retroflex (i.e. apico-postalveolar) fricative.

AMERICAN USAGE

Not used. [ʂ] would be used instead.

SOURCE

Roman alphabet lower-case *s*, with the IPA's rightward tail diacritic for retroflex consonants.

ESH

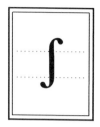

IPA USAGE

Voiceless palato-alveolar central laminal fricative.

AMERICAN USAGE

Generally not used, ⟨š⟩ being used instead.

SOURCE

A modified ⟨s⟩. Similar to the "long *s*" of early English printers' fonts. It occurs in this form with this value in Isaac Pitman's 1845 Phonotypic alphabet (cf. Pitman and St. John 1969, 82), where it functions as the (invented) lower-case print form of a Greek capital sigma.

Double-barred Esh

IPA Usage: Not used. *American Usage:* Not used; the occurrence in Chomsky and Halle 1968 (p. 320) is in the context of a reference to Beach 1938. *Source:* Invented by D. M. Beach (1938, 289), modifying the previously established symbol ⟨≠⟩ (q.v.) for a "denti-alveolar implosive" click consonant. Beach states (1938, 77–78) that the symbol has been "derived from the symbol in current use by adding curves to the ends of the upright traversal in order to conform in general style and appearance to the other phonetic symbols employed by the International Phonetic Association" and adds: "I am recommending the symbol ǂ for official adoption by the I.P.A."

Apparently his recommendation was never officially accepted, for double-barred esh did not appear in the 1949 or 1979 charts, or even merit a mention in the "Further Improvements" section of *Principles* (p. 19). Beach suggests ⟨ ꭓ ⟩ for the nasalized variety.

Reversed Esh with Top Loop

IPA Usage: Recommended in *Principles* (p. 14) for a labialized variety of [ʃ] or [ç], i.e. voiceless palato-alveolar or palatal fricative with lip-rounding. This symbol is recommended for the sound in Twi represented orthographically as *hw* before [i], [e], and [ɛ], though in fact it is not used in the Twi text transcribed in *Principles*, (p. 46): [hɥ] is used instead. Approval of the symbol was withdrawn in 1976 (*JIPA* 6.1, 3) in favor of equivalent digraphs such as [ʃʷ], [çʷ], and [hɥ].

CURLY-TAIL ESH

IPA USAGE

Palatalized voiceless palato-alveolar central fricative. Equivalent to [ʃʲ]. Rarely found.

AMERICAN USAGE

Not used.

SOURCE

Esh, modified with clockwise curly tail.

LOWER-CASE T

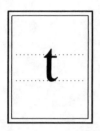

IPA USAGE

Voiceless alveolar or dental stop.

AMERICAN USAGE

Same as IPA.

COMMENTS

Note variants: [t̪] (dental), [t'] (ejective), [tʷ] (labialized), etc.

The logical extension of the fricative symbol-forming cross (cf. *Crossed D, Crossed G,* etc.) to *t* is [ŧ] which is used in Meillet and Cohen 1952 (p. xiii) for a voiceless dental fricative.

SOURCE

Roman alphabet, lower case.

T with Upper Left Hook

IPA Usage: Not used. The official transcription is [ʈ]. *American Usage:* Not used. [ʈ] would generally be used. *Other uses:* Used by Daniel Jones in early transcriptions to indicate a voiceless retroflex stop, in particular for Sinhalese. According to Jones, the IPA symbol [ʈ] was introduced in 1927 (see Jones and Laver [1983, 202, n. 36]), replacing this character and the traditional [t]. An arbitrary modification of ⟨t⟩.

LEFT-HOOK T

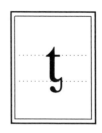

IPA USAGE

Palatalized voiceless alveolar or dental stop. Equivalent to [tʲ].

AMERICAN USAGE

Not used. The digraph [tʸ] would generally be used instead.

COMMENTS

As in Russian [pjatʲ] 'five'.

SOURCE

Roman alphabet lower-case *t*, with the left-facing hook (q.v.) that the
IPA uses for consonants denoting palatalized sounds.

T WITH RIGHT TAIL

IPA USAGE

Voiceless retroflex (i.e. apico-postalveolar) stop.

AMERICAN USAGE

Not normally used; [ʈ] is used instead.

COMMENTS

As in the sound represented by Hindi ⟨ ड ⟩.

The retroflexion diacritic used by the IPA in [ʂ] and [ʐ] is echoed by the rightward-swept elongation of the rightmost vertical stroke of a character in the IPA's special symbols for other retroflex consonants: [ɳ], [ɭ], [ɖ], and [ɽ]. In the interest of terminological consistency, we recognize in this family resemblance an IPA retroflexion indicator which we call "right-tail" (q.v.).

SOURCE

Roman alphabet lower-case *t*, modified by the incorporation of the IPA diacritic for retroflexion.

T-ESH LIGATURE

IPA USAGE

Voiceless palato-aveolar affricate.

AMERICAN USAGE

Not generally used; [tš] or [č] would be used instead.

SOURCE

A ligature of ⟨t⟩ and ⟨ʃ⟩. A palato-alveolar affricate has an alveolar stop component (hence the ⟨t⟩) and a palato-alveolar fricative offglide (hence the ⟨ʃ⟩).

TURNED T

IPA USAGE

Voiceless velaric ingressive dental stop (i.e. dental click).

AMERICAN USAGE

Not used.

OTHER USES

Used in some very early work by Dorsey on Ponca (Siouan) to represent unaspirated [t] so that ⟨t⟩ could be used for the aspirated [tʰ] (see Boas and Swanton 1911, 881).

Beach (1938, 289) uses the symbol with its IPA interpretation and suggests [ꞁ] for the nasal variety of the click.

COMMENTS

As illustrated by the noise of disapproval usually represented by "tut-tut" in novelists' representations of English dialogue.

SOURCE

Roman alphabet lower-case *t*, turned (rotated 180°).

THETA

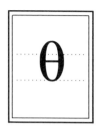

IPA USAGE

Voiceless interdental central fricative.

AMERICAN USAGE

Same as IPA (but see comments about script theta below).

COMMENTS

It is very important to distinguish ⟨θ⟩ from ⟨ө⟩ (barred *o*) if the latter is used.

It is also important to distinguish ⟨θ⟩ from the rarely found script version of the letter, ⟨ϑ⟩. Boas et al. (1916, 5) proposed that script theta should be used for voiced interdental fricatives, IPA [ð], and very occasionally this may be found in Americanist literature (see e.g. Spier 1946, 17). However, ⟨ð⟩ has since become standard among Americanists as it has among almost all linguists.

SOURCE

Greek alphabet, as printed. *Principles* (p. 2) explicitly rejects the script form ⟨ϑ⟩ which, according to the *Chicago Manual of Style,* Thirteenth Edition, p. 276, is "usually used in mathematical formulas" and "should not be combined with other fonts." Theta represents IPA [θ] in Modern Greek.

 Barred O
See page 113.

 Thorn
See page 128.

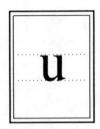

LOWER-CASE U

IPA USAGE

Cardinal vowel No. 8: high back rounded.

AMERICAN USAGE

Same as IPA.

COMMENTS

As in French *ou* 'or'.

SOURCE

Roman alphabet, lower case.

U with Over-dot

IPA Usage: Not used.   *American Usage:* Not in general use. Following the recommendations of Boas et al. (1916, 10) on the use of the over-dot diacritic (q.v.) as an indicator for central vowels, used by Bloch and Trager (1942, 22) for a high central rounded vowel (IPA [ʉ]). Trager (1964, 16) suggests this and [u] as alternatives.

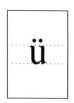

U Umlaut

IPA Usage: According to *Principles* (p. 16), a high central rounded vowel, an alternative to [ʉ] recommended for use when the sound is clearly a member of a back vowel phoneme /u/. The current interpretation of the umlaut diacritic (q.v.) makes [ü] a central*ized* high back round vowel between [u] and [ʉ]. *American Usage:* According to the widely followed recommendation of Boas et al. (1916, 9) on the use of the umlaut (q.v.) with vowel symbols, [ü] represents a rounded high front vowel, i.e. a vowel with all of the properties of [u] but front instead of back. The IPA transcription would be [y]. Cf. Bloch and Trager (1942, 22), Trager (1964, 16), Pike (1947, 5), Gleason (1955, 8), Smalley (1963, 309). A case of almost total unanimity among American phoneticians on a usage that directly conflicts with the IPA. The IPA transcription for a high front rounded vowel is [y], which is occasionally found in American works and is acknowledged to be "in common use" by Bloch and Trager (1942, 21). *Comments:* The result of the change in the IPA's interpretation of the umlaut and its common use in a different sense in American practice is a rather confusing situation in which [ü] may denote a centralized back vowel (official IPA), a central vowel (*Principles*), or a front vowel (e.g. Bloch and Trager). *Source:* The character is used in German orthography to denote a high front rounded vowel.

BARRED U

IPA USAGE

High central rounded vowel, between Cardinal 1 and Cardinal 8.

AMERICAN USAGE

Same as IPA where used, as e.g. by Pike (1947, 5).

A high central rounded vowel could be transcribed as [ů], using the over-dot diacritic (q.v.) suggested by Boas et al. (1916, 10).

COMMENTS

The sound [ʉ] is heard in Norwegian words such as *hus,* and in Scottish pronunciations of English words like *good.* (Note the novelist's device of writing the word as *guid* to indicate this vowel quality.)

Neither Smalley 1963 nor Halle and Clements 1983 give symbols for any central rounded vowels, and Gleason 1955 gives barred *u* as denoting a high back unrounded vowel (IPA [ɯ]). The omission of central rounded vowels from the phonetic charts of so many phonologists may indicate not an oversight but rather a tacit phonological hypothesis that a three-way backness distinction in rounded vowels cannot exist in a language. This becomes explicit in Chomsky and Halle (1968, 315), where it is suggested that the [y]/[ʉ] distinction in Swedish is not a function of the feature [back] but of the feature [covered], which relates to constriction of the pharynx and is independent of backness.

SOURCE

Roman alphabet lower-case *u,* modified with superimposed hyphen.

Half-barred U

IPA Usage: Not used.   *American Usage:* Not in use, but proposed by Trager (1964, 16) for a high central rounded vowel, an alternative to the [ʉ] of Bloch and Trager (1942, 22). A Trager suggestion that never caught on. The equivalent IPA transcription is [ʉ], but Trager has this for a high *front* rounded vowel.

Slashed U

Might be encountered as a typographical alternant of ⟨ʉ⟩; see e.g. Chistovich et al. (1982, 171).

UPSILON

IPA USAGE

Semi-high back rounded vowel, between Cardinal 7 and Cardinal 8; approved alternative to ⟨ɷ⟩ (*Principles*, 8).

AMERICAN USAGE

Same as IPA, though [U] is common.

COMMENTS

The vowel in English *put, cook.*

   The symbol ⟨ʊ⟩ must be distinguished from the IPA's ⟨ʋ⟩, *Script v* (q.v.), which denotes a labiodental frictionless continuant. Note that Smalley's upsilon looks more like ⟨ʋ⟩ than ⟨ʊ⟩.

SOURCE

Roughly like the Greek alphabet lower-case upsilon. Typographically, the character in *Principles* (p. 8, n. 1) may be, and the one in (e.g.) Tucker (1971, 648) clearly is, a turned (rotated 180°) small capital Omega.

Small Capital U

IPA Usage: Not used, except perhaps as a typographical substitute for upsilon (⟨ʊ⟩).   *American Usage:* Semi-high back rounded vowel, IPA [ɷ], between Cardinals 7 and 8.   Boas et al. (1916, 10) recommend that small capital letters be used for the voiceless versions of normally voiced sounds and hence [ʊ] could be found for a voiceless [u], IPA [u̥]. Its use for the semi-high back rounded vowel is far more common.

Small Capital U with Over-dot

IPA Usage: Not used. *American Usage:* Not in general use. Following the recommendation of Boas et al. (1916, 10) on the use of the over-dot diacritic (q.v.) for central vowels, used by Bloch and Trager (1942, 22) for a lower-high central rounded vowel. Trager (1964, 16) suggests this symbol or ⟨ᵾ⟩ as alternatives. The equivalent *Principles* transcription is [ö̤] or [ÿ].

Barred Small Capital U

IPA Usage: Not used. *American Usage:* Not in use, but proposed by Trager (1964, 16) for a high front rounded vowel, as an alternative to the [ü] of Bloch and Trager (1942, 22). A Trager suggestion that never caught on. The equivalent IPA transcription is [y].

Turned Small Capital U

Used by Samarin (1967, 182) for a "mean-mid" back rounded vowel, in place of Trager's small capital omega, [Ω]. Used in Crothers (1978, 137) for a higher-low back rounded vowel (IPA[ɔ⊤]) instead of Bloch and Trager's [ω].

Capital U

Boas et al. (1916, 10) recommend the use of small capitals to represent the voiceless versions of normally voiced sounds (either vowels or sonorants). Pike 1947 and Smalley 1963 both suggest the use of capital letters for voiceless vowels; thus the transcription [U] might be used for IPA [u̥]. Not frequently found.

Turned M
See page 97.

Turned M with Long Right Leg
See page 98.

LOWER-CASE V

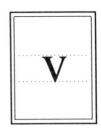

IPA USAGE
Voiced labiodental fricative.

AMERICAN USAGE
Same as IPA.

COMMENTS

The letter *v* represents [v] in English orthography but not in all Roman-based orthographies; in Spanish, for example, it has both [b] and [β] as possible values.

The letter *v* is often used by phonologists to indicate an arbitrary vowel. Most often, the symbol used (as in "CV syllable structure" for consonant-vowel syllable structure) is upper-case *V*, which has no phonetic use, but a lower-case *v* might occasionally be found used in this way. (We have been told that early Iroquoianists used *v* to represent a neutral central low vowel, but have not been able to locate an instance of this in print.)

SOURCE

Roman alphabet, lower case.

SCRIPT V

IPA USAGE

Voiced labiodental frictionless continuant.

AMERICAN USAGE

Not generally used; but Gleason gives ⟨ʋ⟩ for IPA ⟨β⟩, a voiced bilabial fricative. Script *v* is used with its IPA value in Kurath 1939 (p. 140).

COMMENTS

The IPA interpretation represents the initial sound of Hindi *woo* 'he/she'.

Must be distinguished from [ʊ] (upsilon).

Used in the International African Institute's standard African alphabet for a voiced bilabial fricative, IPA [β], and hence in some phonetics texts, cf. Westermann and Ward (1933).

Used by Ladefoged (1968, 25f) for a voiced bilabial approximant without strong lip rounding, as found in Bini, Esoko, and other Edo languages of West Africa.

SOURCE

Roman alphabet lower-case *v* as in some styles of handwriting.

Λ *Inverted v*
    See page 18.

LOWER-CASE W

Voiced rounded labiovelar approximant.

Same as IPA.

As a right superscript (or, under a seldom-followed IPA recommendation, in a cursive form as a centered subscript), *w* indicates labialization of a consonant.

The letter *w* does not represent [w] in all Roman-based orthographies; in Welsh, for example, it represents [ʊ], and in German, Polish, and other languages, it represents [v].

J. R. Firth used ⟨w⟩ to represent [ʊ] in his "All-India" alphabet, which is employed in a number of works on Indian languages; see e.g. Harley (1944, xiii), Bailey et al. (1956, xv).

Ladefoged uses [w⊥] for a voiced rounded labiovelar fricative (1968, 25).

Roman alphabet, lower case.

Subscript W

IPA Usage: As a centered subscript, indicates labialization of a consonant; thus [t̫] is a voiceless alveolar stop with lip rounding. In practice its use as a right superscript (e.g. [tʷ]) is more common. The IPA's choice of typographical shape suggests a subscript lower-case omega rather than *w*, but it seems sensible to call it a *w* nonetheless.

W with Over-dot

IPA Usage: According to IPA conventions (*Principles*, 17), this would represent a palatalized bilabial semivowel (glide); in other words, [ɥ]. *American Usage:* Not in general use. Following the recommendation of Boas et al. (1916, 10) for the use of the over-dot (q.v.) as a diacritic for central vowels, Trager (1964, 16) uses [ẇ] for a central rounded semivowel. The *Principles*-type transcription corresponding to Trager's [ẇ] is [ɥ] or [ẅ].

W Umlaut

IPA Usage: Assuming the umlaut diacritic can be applied to semi-vowels (i.e. glides) as well as vowels, according to *Principles* (p. 16) a central rounded semivowel, i.e. a semivowel of [ʉ] quality. In 1976 the IPA altered the definition of the umlaut diacritic (q.v.) so that it marks a vowel as "centralized," not central (*JIPA* 6, 2). Under this interpretation, [ẅ] would represent a centralized rounded semi-vowel. *American Usage:* Not generally used, but proposed by Trager (1964, 16), following the recommendations of Boas et al. (1916, 9) on the use of the umlaut diacritic, for a front rounded semi-vowel, IPA [ɥ]. Cf. Meillet and Cohen (1952, xiii) for a use with this sense. *Comments:* The result of the change in the IPA's interpretation of the umlaut and its common use with a different sense in American practice is a rather confusing situation in which [ẅ] might denote a centralized back semivowel (official IPA), a central semi-vowel (*Principles*) or a front semivowel (e.g. Trager).

Slashed W

Used by Monzón and Seneff (1984, 456n) for a sound observed in certain Nahuatl dialects, described as "characterized by the parallel position of lips (as for [ƀ]) and a velar onglide—no friction has been noted." Perhaps, therefore, a voiced, unrounded, labiovelar approximant: a variety of [γ͡β] without friction, in IPA terms, and perhaps a variety of the sound for which Ladefoged suggested [ɰ], with added labial constriction.

INVERTED W

IPA USAGE

Voiceless rounded labiovelar approximant or fricative (i.e. devoiced [w]).

AMERICAN USAGE

Not used.

COMMENTS

Designed as a single-symbol representation of the sound written *wh* in those English dialects which distinguish *which* from *witch*.

SOURCE

Roman alphabet lower-case *w*, vertically inverted. The character is distinct from small capital *m*.

ω *Lower-case Omega*
See page 121.

ധ *Closed Omega*
See page 125.

ρ *Wynn*
See page 127.

LOWER-CASE X

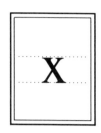

IPA USAGE

Voiceless velar fricative.

AMERICAN USAGE

Same as IPA.

OTHER USES

Since ⟨x⟩ represents [ç] in many New World varieties of Spanish (note the pronunciation [meçiko] for *Mexico*) and represents [ʃ] in Portuguese, it commonly denotes a palatal or palato-alveolar voiceless fricative in Central and South American transcriptions. It also represents a palatal or "alveolopalatal" fricative (IPA [ç] or [ɕ]) in the Pinyin transliteration of Mandarin Chinese.

COMMENTS

The values that *x* has in English orthography, namely [z] initially and [ks] or [gz] elsewhere, have no connection to any recognized use of ⟨x⟩ in phonetic transcription and should be ignored.

This symbol must be carefully distinguished from [χ], Greek chi, which denotes a uvular fricative rather than a velar one.

Smalley 1963 does not recognize uvular obstruents per se, calling them "backed velars," and uses [x̣] for a voiceless "backed velar" fricative.

SOURCE

Cyrillic alphabet. While ⟨x⟩ has various values in Roman-based Western European orthographies, in the Eastern European languages written with the Greek-derived Cyrillic alphabet (e.g. in Russian and Bulgarian), the letter with this shape denotes a voiceless velar fricative.

X with Subscript Circumflex

IPA Usage: Not used.   *American Usage:* Given by Smalley (1963, 455) for a voiceless palatal central fricative, i.e. IPA [ç], corresponding to the [x̱] of Pike (1947, 7) and Gleason (1955, 7).

X with Subscript Arch

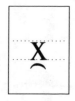

IPA Usage: Not used.   *American Usage:* Used by Pike (1947, 7) and Gleason (1955, 7) for a voiceless palatal central fricative, i.e. IPA [ç], corresponding to the [x̭] of Smalley (1963, 455).

Upper-case X

Not standard, but may sometimes be found to indicate a voiceless uvular fricative, IPA [χ] (see e.g. Hyman 1975, 241).

CHI

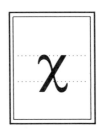

IPA USAGE

Voiced uvular central fricative.

AMERICAN USAGE

Same as IPA, if used, but alternatives such as [x] are also found.

Following the terminology of Boas et al. (1916, 4), Pike and Smalley do not recognize uvular obstruents as such, calling them "back[ed] velars," and using [x] for a voiceless "backed velar" fricative.

COMMENTS

Heard in some pronunciations of French words like *lettre* and *liberté,* where a uvular *r* is devoiced.

SOURCE

Greek chi. It represents a back fricative in Greek (but a velar one, not a uvular one).

LOWER-CASE Y

Cardinal vowel No. 9: high front rounded. The secondary cardinal vowel corresponding to Cardinal 1.

AMERICAN USAGE

Voiced unrounded palatal central approximant (IPA [j]).

OTHER USES

Slavicists use ⟨y⟩ to represent a high central or back unrounded vowel, IPA [ɨ] or [ɯ], as in the standard romanization for Russian.

J. R. Firth used ⟨y⟩ for both [ɩ] and [j] in his "All-India" alphabet, which is used in a number of works on Indian languages; see e.g. Harley (1944, xii–xvi), Bailey et al. (1956, xv–xvi). The ambiguity here is not pernicious, since [ɩ] and [j] are in complementary distribution in the languages in question.

COMMENTS

The usage of the transcription [y] is perhaps the single most salient example of a problematic divergence between American and European transcription practices. It is unfortunate that the IPA's recommendation has not influenced the American community, which uses ⟨y⟩ for [j] when transcribing English and for [ɨ] when transliterating Slavic languages, making ⟨y⟩ ambiguous in three ways. As things stand, the literature contains many traps set for the unwary. For example, "[y]" on p. 315 of Chomsky and Halle (1968) denotes IPA [y], but the "[y]" on p. 316, the very next page, denotes IPA [j].

It is crucial to be aware of the background of the writer when interpreting an unexplained occurrence of '[y]'. Yet mere geographical provenance cannot be relied upon simplistically; for example, Kurath (1939, 123), writing in the United States, uses ⟨y⟩ with its IPA meaning.

Matters become even more complex if one takes orthographic usages of *y* into consideration: it represents [j], [i], or [ɪ] in English orthography, [ə] or [ʊ] in Welsh orthography, [ɨ] in Polish orthography, and so on—though it does generally represent a high front rounded vowel in German.

The coexistence of the IPA and other uses of ⟨y⟩ (and hence ⟨j⟩) is recognized within the IPA community to be an ongoing problem. *Principles* notes that the "World Orthography" described in the International African Institute's *Practical Orthography for African Languages* and widely used for African languages differs from the IPA *only* in that "*j* and *y* are taken to have their English consonantal values." Despite a general recognition by the council of the IPA that the situation regarding [j] (q.v.) and [y] is undesirably confused, and considerable support for moving to the American interpretation of [y], resolution of the problem was deferred in 1976 (*JIPA* 6, 2–3) with the council split on whether to retain [j] as a palatal approximant or to use [y] instead.

SOURCE

Roman alphabet, lower case. IPA usage follows Old English and some other Germanic languages, but is at odds with English and many other orthographies.

Superscript Y

IPA Usage: If used, would indicate coloration of [y] quality, i.e. modification in the direction of high, front, rounded articulation. Could be used, perhaps, to narrowly transcribe the *l* of French *lui:* (lʸɥi]. *American Usage:* Indicates palatalization, as recommended by Herzog et al. (1934, 630), or (with an alveolar consonant symbol) palato-alveolar articulation; thus Pike's (1947) [lʸ] denotes a palato-alveolar lateral approximant; the IPA transcription would be [lʲ].

Y Umlaut

IPA Usage: According to *Principles* (p. 16), a high central rounded vowel, i.e. equivalent to [ʉ], though the revised interpretation of the umlaut (q.v.) diacritic would make [ÿ] represent a central*ized* (i.e. somewhat retracted) front rounded vowel.   *American Usage:* Not in general use, but proposed by Trager (1964, 16) (following the recommendations of Boas et al. [1916, 9] on the use of the umlaut diacritic) for a back unrounded semivowel, as an alternative to IPA [ɰ]. *Comments:* The result of the IPA's interpretation of the umlaut diacritic and its common use with a different sense in American practice is a rather confusing situation in which y with an umlaut diacritic could be interpreted as denoting a centralized high front vowel (official IPA), a high central rounded vowel (*Principles*), or a back unrounded semivowel (Trager).

TURNED Y

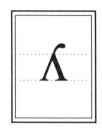

IPA USAGE

Voiced palatal lateral approximant.

AMERICAN USAGE

Same as IPA.

COMMENTS

As represented by *gl* in Italian and *ll* in Castilian Spanish.

SOURCE

Roman alphabet lower-case y, turned (rotated 180°). Visually suggestive of a laterally reversed Greek lambda. Also suggestive of y—misleadingly, perhaps, since a palatal lateral approximant sounds a lot like the palatal central approximant [j], and *y* represents [j] in some orthographies, but not in the IPA system.

SMALL CAPITAL Y

IPA USAGE

Semi-high front rounded vowel, i.e. rounded counterpart of [ɪ].

AMERICAN USAGE

Not generally used. Bloch and Trager (1942, 22) and sources following them use [ʊ] for rounded [ɪ].

OTHER USES

Boas et al. (1916, 10) recommend that small capital letters be used for the voiceless versions of normally voiced sounds; since American [y] is a voiced unrounded palatal central approximant, small capital *y* would represent a voiceless unrounded palatal central approximant.

COMMENTS

The vowel sound in German *fünf, Glück*.

SOURCE

Roman alphabet, small capital font; [ʏ] is to [y] as [ɪ] (or [ɪ]) is to [i].

Turned H
See page 71.

Lambda
See page 94.

LOWER-CASE Z

IPA USAGE

Voiced alveolar or dental central fricative.

AMERICAN USAGE

Same as IPA.

COMMENTS

An obvious choice to represent [z] for speakers of English, but not necessarily for speakers of other languages with Roman-based orthographies; *z* stands for [ts] in German, [θ] in Castilian Spanish, and [s] in Basque, Catalan, and New World Spanish.

Note that some diacritics indicate a more radical change of denotation: [ž] is the American transcription for a voiced alveopalatal fricative, IPA [ʒ], [ź] is used in the Polish orthography and some comparative studies for a voiced laminal palatal fricative, IPA [ʑ] (*Principles*, 12).

An upper case *z* has been used by some Indo-Europeanists to represent "a laryngeal not retained in Hittite" (see Hamp 1965a, 123, n. 3), but we have not regarded this as meriting a separate entry for capital *z*.

SOURCE

Roman alphabet, lower case.

Comma-tail Z

Found in grammars of Old High German representing the reflex of Proto-Germanic non-initial *t* after the Second Consonant Shift (see e.g. Ellis 1953, 21 etc.; Wright 1910, 54 etc.; Prokosch 1939, 81). It is not clear what its phonetic value was, but it is generally agreed that it was some sort of dental fricative, and that it had collapsed with [s] by the end of the Middle High German period. See Brauner (1967, 12, 85). The symbol is quite specific to work on Old High German, and should not be regarded as a phonetic symbol for general use. Prokosch (1939, 81) has it as ⟨z̦⟩, hence our name for it.

Z WEDGE

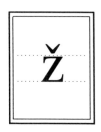

IPA USAGE

Not used.

AMERICAN USAGE

Generally used in place of the IPA [ʒ] for a voiced palato-alveolar central laminal fricative.

COMMENTS

The recommendations of Herzog et al. (1934, 631) on the use of the wedge diacritic in characters for palato-alveolar consonants required the substitution of [ž] for the earlier Americanist use of [ǰ]. The recommendation has been almost universally followed. Herzog et al. recommended the yogh symbol for a voiced alveolar affricate.

Brugmann (1904, 1) uses ⟨ž⟩ with the value IPA [ʒ].

SOURCE

Roman alphabet lower-case *z*, with wedge diacritic, as used in the Czech orthography. The diacritic is called the *háček* ('little hook') in Czech and called "wedge" by many American linguists.

CURLY-TAIL Z

IPA USAGE

Voiced "alveolo-palatal" central laminal fricative. Articulated further forward than [j] (true palatal) but not as far forward as [ʒ] (palato-alveolar), and articulated laminally (with the flat blade of the tongue) rather than apically (with the tip of the tongue, as in [ʐ], retroflex).

AMERICAN USAGE

Listed by Halle and Clements (1983, 29) as a voiced palatal central fricative, i.e. IPA [j]. Usually not used by American phoneticians.

COMMENTS

Illustrated, according to *Principles* (p. 12), by the sound represented as ⟨ź⟩ in Polish *źle*.

The IPA's distinction between "alveolo-palatal" place of articulation (closer to palatal) and palato-alveolar (closer to alveolar) has not gained wide currency. The term palato-alveolar is standard, but the term "alveolo-palatal" is not, and in fact is rarely encountered. The term "alveopalatal" used by Gleason, Pike, and Smalley corresponds to the IPA's palato-alveolar.

SOURCE

Roman alphabet lower-case *z* (used for a voiced alveolar fricative) modified with the same curly tail used in ⟨ç⟩ (IPA voiceless "alveolo-palatal" central fricative).

Z WITH RIGHT TAIL

IPA USAGE

Voiced retroflex (i.e. apico-postalveolar) fricative.

AMERICAN USAGE

Not used. [ʐ] would be used instead.

SOURCE

Roman alphabet lower-case *z*, with the IPA's rightward tail diacritic for retroflex consonants.

YOGH

IPA USAGE

Voiced palato-alveolar central laminal fricative.

AMERICAN USAGE

Generally not used ([ž] being used instead). Recommended by Herzog et al. (1934, 631) to represent [dz] when it occurs as a single affricate consonant, but this usage is now not common.

OTHER USES

Some Slavicists use ⟨ʒ⟩ for IPA [dz]; this is the origin of the Herzog et al. recommendation, and it may be exhibited elsewhere in linguistic works; thus, for example, the reference to "[ǯ] and [ʒ]" by Kiparsky (1968, 183) means IPA [dʒ] and [dz] respectively. Note also Hoijer (1945, 12), where [ʒ] is used for the "voiceless, lenis, and un-aspirated" alveolar affricate of Navaho, IPA [ḓz̥].

SOURCE

This Old Irish form of *g* was used in Old English orthography to represent, at various times, a voiced velar stop, a voiced velar fricative, and a palatal approximant. It survived into Middle English with the latter two values in the form ⟨ʒ⟩ and called "yogh." It is sometimes found set as ⟨ʒ⟩ (cf. Jones 1972). The letter was used in Scotland later than in England and English printers perceived a similarity between the ⟨ʒ⟩ form and a form of *z* and substituted the latter. This led, according to Jespersen (1949, 22), to the current spelling pronunciation of Scottish names like *Mackenzie*. The character occurs in this form with this value in Isaac Pitman's 1845 Phonotypic alphabet (cf. Pitman and St. John 1969, 82).

Yogh Wedge

IPA Usage: Not used. *American Usage:* The recommendations of Herzog et al. (1934, 631) which formalized the use of the wedge diacritic in American transcription used this character for a voiced palato-alveolar affricate consonant, IPA [dʒ]. The regular analogic pattern of their recommendations was interrupted by the replacement of [ǯ] by [ǰ], presumably for considerations of typographical ease. Cf. Hoijer (1945, 8), who uses a transcription which is otherwise consistent with previous recommendations except in the use of ⟨ǰ⟩ for ⟨ǯ⟩. Cf. also Bloomfield (1933, 129), who uses ⟨ǰ⟩ for IPA [dʒ]. *Other uses:* Some Slavicists use ⟨ǯ⟩ for IPA [dʒ]; this is the origin of the Herzog et al. recommendation, and it may be exhibited elsewhere in linguistic works; thus, for example, the reference to "[ǯ] and [ʒ]" by Kiparsky (1968, 183) means IPA [dʒ] and [dz] respectively. *Source:* The character is yogh (q.v. above) with the wedge diacritic called *haček* ('little hook') or wedge used for certain palato-alveolar consonants in the Czech orthography.

Bent-tail Yogh

IPA Usage: Recommended (*Principles,* 14) for a labialized variety of [ʒ] or [j], i.e. voiced palato-alveolar or palatal fricative with lip-rounding. Equivalent to [ʒʷ] or [jʷ]. Recommended for the sound represented orthographically as ⟨w⟩ before [i], [e], and [ɛ] in Twi (though the character is not used in the Twi sample [p. 46]). Approval was withdrawn in 1976 (*JIPA* 6, 3) in favor of the equivalent digraph. *American Usage:* Not used. *Comments:* Rarely if ever used, even during the period of its being sanctioned by the IPA. The occurrence in Pike (1943, 75) in a quotation from Kenyon is spurious; it is a typesetter's error in quoting Kenyon's use of reversed epsilon with the rhotacization hook.

CURLY-TAIL YOGH

IPA USAGE

Palatalized voiced palato-alveolar central fricative. Equivalent to [ʒʲ].

AMERICAN USAGE

Not used.

COMMENTS

Rarely found.

SOURCE

Yogh, modified with clockwise curly tail.

Crossed Two

IPA Usage: Recommended in *Principles* (p. 15) for a voiced alveolar affricate with central fricative release. Equivalent to [dz]. Given in case a single letter is needed for the voiced alveolar affricate where it patterns as a single segment. IPA approval was withdrawn in 1976 in favor of digraphs and ligatures (*JIPA* 6, 3). An arbitrary invention, vaguely reminiscent of *z* in shape.   *American Usage:* Not used. For similar purposes, Herzog et al. (1934, 631) recommended ⟨Ʒ⟩ for IPA [dz].

Turned Two

IPA Usage: A proposed (*Principles*, 19) character for the voiceless pharyngeal fricative but not officially approved. The character is the numeral 2 turned (rotated 180°). An IPA invention suggestive of the Arabic character ⟨ ⟩ (*ḥa*). *American Usage:* Not used.

Turned Three

IPA Usage: A proposed (*Principles*, 19) but not officially approved character for the voiced pharyngeal fricative (standard IPA [ʕ]). *American Usage:* Not used. *Comments:* The character in *Principles* is clearly a turned (rotated 180°) *three* in its rounded form, i.e. ⟨3⟩, which is visually suggestive of the Arabic character for the sound, ⟨ ɛ ⟩ (*'ain*). A reversed curved yogh would typographically look very much like a turned ⟨3⟩. Cf. Meillet and Cohen (1952, xiii). The character used by Firth (1948, 142) for IPA [ʕ] (see below) is typographically ambiguous between a reversed *yogh* and a laterally reversed *three* with a flat top, i.e. ⟨ꝫ⟩.

Reversed Yogh

Used by Firth (1948) to represent the *'ain* (⟨ ɛ ⟩) of Arabic (IPA [ʕ]), apparently following an established tradition. Perhaps intended to be the turned *3* (q.v.) unofficially suggested by the IPA (*Principles,* 19). Firth also uses ⟨ʕ⟩ for Arabic *hamza* ⟨ ʾ ⟩ (see Firth 1948, 142, 147–49). Clearly, visual similarity between Arabic ⟨ ɛ ⟩ and the laterally reversed yogh is the motivation for this use of the symbol.

Seven

Used in practical orthographies for Mayan languages to represent the glottal stop, IPA [ʔ]. Cf. Kaufman (1976, 25). It is useful in that it is vaguely suggestive of the glottal stop symbol in shape and is available on an unmodified typewriter, but distinct from punctuation marks.

Nine with Subscript Tilde

Smalley's suggestion (1963, 444) for a voiced pharyngealized vowel glide, i.e. the Arabic *'ain* sound, IPA [ʕ]. Smalley uses a subscript tilde to indicate pharyngealization. According to Smalley, this symbol is "arbitrary" but "does have the advantage that the English word *nine* sounds something like the Arabic word *ayin* for anyone who happens to remember it"!

Null Sign

This symbol has no phonetic value, but is used by phonologists to notate a zero morpheme, or to indicate nothing—e.g. to show the effect of a deletion, or to represent epenthesis rules as replacement of nothing by some specified segment. Dinnsen (1974, p. 43), for example, uses ⟨∅⟩ as the notation for a phonological segment "specified minus for all features" and thus not endowed with any phonetic properties, and argues that this null segment nonetheless plays a role in the phonology of some languages.

Mentioning the null sign here allows us to stress that it is distinct from all four of the following visually rather similar characters: *Phi* (⟨Φ⟩), *Barred o* (⟨ө⟩), *Slashed o* (⟨ø⟩) and *Theta* (⟨θ⟩). Typesetting errors in connection with these symbols are unfortunately fairly common.

I *Undotted I*
   See page 74.

Ɜ *Reversed Epsilon*
   See page 52.

Ʒ *Yogh*
   See page 178.

GLOTTAL STOP

IPA USAGE

Glottal stop.

AMERICAN USAGE

Same as IPA.

COMMENTS

Sometimes the question mark, ⟨?⟩, is used as a typographical substitute. Note also that differing fonts may have different-looking symbols for the glottal stop. For example:

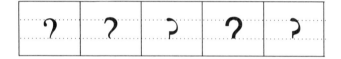

The ⟨ ʔ ⟩ listed for the glottal plosive at the beginning of the second edition of Gimson (1970, ix) is a printer's error. The first (1962) and third (1980) editions are correct.

SOURCE

Question mark with dot removed and (in some fonts) leg lengthened.

Superscript Glottal Stop

IPA Usage: Not used.   *American Usage:* Used as a diacritic with symbols for voiceless stops to form symbols for ejective or glottalized consonants, either over the symbols or as a right superscript. Used over vowels by Smalley (1963, 389ff) to represent laryngealization.

Question Mark

Occasionally found as a more easily typed and typeset version of ⟨ʔ⟩, denoting a glottal stop.

INVERTED GLOTTAL STOP

IPA USAGE

Velaric ingressive alveolar laterally released stop (i.e. lateral click).

AMERICAN USAGE

Same as IPA, if used.

COMMENTS

Represents a sound similar to the sound used (within large segments of the English-speaking community) to gee up a horse. Found as a consonant in most Bushman languages and in some Southern Bantu languages. Represented by *x* in the Zulu orthography.

Beach (1938, 289) gives ⟨ ɓ ⟩ for the nasal correspondent of the sound.

SOURCE

Invention of the IPA. Vertically inverted glottal stop symbol (with an extended leg), or ⟨ʖ⟩ with top cross-bar removed. The character in Ladefoged 1971 (p. 23) is clearly an inverted glottal stop.

Crossed Inverted Glottal Stop

ƨ

IPA Usage: Recommended (*Principles*, 15) for a voiceless alveolar affricate with central fricative release in case a single letter is needed for the voiceless alveolar affricate where it patterns as a single segment; for example, the Georgian plain [ts] and ejective [ts'] can be transcribed [ƨ],[ƨ ']. IPA approval was withdrawn in 1976 in favor of the equivalent digraphs and ligatures (*JIPA* 6, 3). An IPA invention. Perhaps a visual compromise between ⟨t⟩ (at the top) and ⟨s⟩ (at the bottom).

REVERSED GLOTTAL STOP

IPA USAGE

Voiced pharyngeal fricative.

AMERICAN USAGE

Same as IPA, if used.

COMMENTS

The Arabic sound traditionally known as *'ain*, written ⟨ ع ⟩ in the Arabic orthography.

There is a confusing usage of this symbol in Firth (1948). Firth uses ⟨ʔ⟩ for the glottal stop in English dialects (see pp. 132, 144–45) but uses ⟨ʕ⟩ for the glottal stop in Arabic (the *hamza*, ⟨ ء ⟩ in the Arabic orthography; see pp. 138–40). For IPA [ʕ], the Arabic *'ain*, he uses ⟨ ε ⟩ (see pp. 142, 147–49). Firth is clearly vacillating between distinct transcription systems: the standard IPA and a variant used for Semitic dialects. (Note the visual similarities: ⟨ʕ⟩, ⟨ ء ⟩, and ⟨ ε ⟩, ⟨ ع ⟩.)

EXCLAMATION POINT

IPA USAGE

Not used.

AMERICAN USAGE

Not standardly used.

OTHER USES

In the South African tradition stemming from 19th century work on the Khoisan languages, often used also by American researchers who have worked on them, [!] represents a velaric ingressive stop (i.e. a click) with an articulation often referred to as palatal, and corresponds to IPA [ʗ]. However, Ladefoged and Traill (1984, 2), departing from most previous work on languages with clicks, describe [!] as an *alveolar* click, disagreeing with earlier writers about what should be considered the primary place of articulation. Caution is necessary, therefore, when this symbol is encountered in future work.

Suggested by Boas et al. (1916, 14), as a diacritic to mark a preceding stop consonant as fortis ("exploded"). It is used throughout the *Handbook of American Indian Languages* (Boas 1910) and other grammars of the period.

Used by some Africanists to mark the "downstep" tone, the distinctive lowering of the tonal register within which other tones take their values. This use is attributed to Daniel Jones by Arnott (1964, 37).

COMMENTS

The click sound denoted by [!] is similar to the pop of a cork being drawn from a bottle. It occurs as a consonant in most Bushman languages and in some Southern Bantu languages. It is represented by *q* in the Zulu orthography.

SOURCE

Due to 19th century orthographic proposals by German philologists, particularly J. G. Krönlein. Cf. Beach (1938, 289).

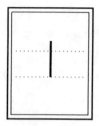

PIPE

IPA USAGE

Not used. The IPA representation for a dental (or alveolar) click is [ǀ].

AMERICAN USAGE

Not standardly used.

OTHER USES

In the South African tradition stemming from 19th century work on the Khoisan languages, often used also by American researchers who have worked on them, represents a velaric ingressive stop (i.e. a click) with dental articulation. Used, for example, throughout Westphal (1971).

Trager and Smith (1951, 45ff) propose an entirely distinct use of the pipe as a representation of "level juncture," indicating the division (juncture) between phrases across which the pitch remains relatively steady, as for example between the items of lists.

COMMENTS

The click transcribed [ǀ] is similar to the sound used in making the disapproving noise commonly written as "tut-tut." It occurs as a consonant in most Khoisan (e.g. Bushman) languages and in some Southern Bantu languages, and is represented as the letter *c* in the Zulu orthography. Ladefoged and Traill (1984, 18) comment: "If it were not for the confusion that would be caused, in view of previous descriptions of clicks, we could more properly call this click dentialveolar, since the contact area at the time of release definitely includes both the upper teeth and the whole of the alveolar ridge." The slash (q.v.) is sometimes used instead of the pipe, giving the transcription '[/]'.

The pipe has occasionally been used by phonologists in an extra-representational way, typically to enclose underlying phonological representations (see e.g. Gruber 1973, 427, fn. 1, for a motley assortment of different uses of pipes and slashes). The expression '‖' for an underlying dental click segment should presumably be avoided in favor of '|/|'.

SOURCE

The symbol is the plain vertical bar used for "Sheffer stroke" in logic and for set definitions (e.g. {x|P(x)}) in mathematics. Trager (1964) calls it "single bar," but we have dubbed it "pipe" (the name current among users of the UNIX computer operating system) in order to avoid an ambiguity about what "bar" means in names like "barred *i.*"

SLASH

IPA USAGE

Not used. The IPA representation for a dental (or alveolar) click is [ǀ].

AMERICAN USAGE

Not standardly used.

OTHER USES

In the South African tradition stemming from 19th century work on the Khoisan languages, often used also by American researchers who have worked on them, represents a velaric ingressive stop (i.e. a click) with dental articulation.

COMMENTS

The consonant represented is similar to the sound used in making the disapproving noise commonly written as "tut-tut." It occurs as a consonant in most Khoisan (e.g. Bushman) languages and in some Southern Bantu languages, and is represented as ⟨c⟩ in the Zulu orthography. Ladefoged and Traill (1984, 18) comment: "If it were not for the confusion that would be caused, in view of previous descriptions of clicks, we could more properly call this click denti-alveolar, since the contact area at the time of release definitely includes both the upper teeth and the whole of the alveolar ridge."

We treat the slash as an acceptable variant form of the vertical bar ⟨ǀ⟩ (herein called "pipe"); it might be regarded as the italic font variety. It is very common to use pipe and slash interchangeably; cf. Ladefoged and Traill (1984), where slash appears in the text but pipe is used in the legend to the diagrams.

Slashes are used by phonologists in a metatranscriptional way to enclose phonemic or other phonological representations, thus: /kæt/

'cat'. The expression '////' for a dental click phoneme should presumably be avoided in favor of '/|/'.

SOURCE

Due to 19th century orthographic proposals by German philologists, particularly J. G. Krönlein (see Beach 1938, 289).

DOUBLE-BARRED PIPE

IPA USAGE

Not used. The IPA does not have a symbol reserved for an alveolar click, but [ǃ] could be used.

AMERICAN USAGE

Not standardly used.

OTHER USES

In the South African tradition stemming from 19th century work on the Khoisan languages, often used also by American researchers who have worked on them, represents a velaric ingressive stop (i.e. a click) with an articulation referred to variously as alveolar and palatal (see comments below).

COMMENTS

Beach asserts that this sound "has been wrongly termed 'palatal' by most writers on Hottentot, including Tindall, Krönlein and Schultze" (1938, 77). But Ladefoged and Traill (1984, 18), after a careful instrumental reinvestigation of this and other clicks, "disagree with Beach in his rejection of the term palatal" for this sound, in effect agreeing with the earlier descriptions (and disagreeing with much other work of this century, e.g. Doke 1926a, 146). They regard the palate as the primary place of articulation, and state that "there is no doubt that [≠] should be described as a palatal sound." Caution is necessary, therefore, when this symbol or the term "palatal click" are encountered in future work, for most modern sources before Ladefoged and Traill agree with Beach.

    The slash is sometimes substituted for the pipe, as it is in the above quotation from Ladefoged and Traill, giving the transcription '[≠]', "Double-barred slash," q.v. below.

Invented during the 19th century, probably by J. G. Krönlein (see Beach 1938, 288ff). Modified to double-barred esh (q.v., p. 143) by Beach (see 1938, 77f).

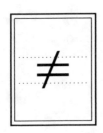

DOUBLE-BARRED SLASH

Not used. The IPA representation for an alveolar (or dental) click is [ǃ].

AMERICAN USAGE

Not standardly used.

OTHER USES

In the South African tradition stemming from 19th century work on the Khoisan languages, often used also by American researchers who have worked on them, represents a velaric ingressive stop (i.e. a click) with an articulation referred to variously as alveolar and palatal (see comments in the previous entry, *Double-barred Pipe*).

COMMENTS

We treat this symbol as an acceptable variant of what we called Double-barred Pipe. It is very clear that the two symbols are regarded as interchangeable; for example, Beach (1938, 77) refers to the "upright transversal" of ⟨≠⟩, as if it contained a vertical bar rather than an oblique stroke.

SOURCE

Invented during the 19th century, probably by J. G. Krönlein (see Beach 1938, 288ff). Basically identical with the "not equal to" sign in mathematics.

DOUBLE PIPE

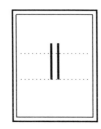

IPA USAGE

Not used. The IPA representation for a lateral click is [ʖ] ("Inverted Glottal Stop," q.v.).

AMERICAN USAGE

Not standardly used.

OTHER USES

In the South African tradition stemming from 19th century work on the Khoisan languages, often used also by American researchers who have worked on them, represents a velaric ingressive stop (i.e. a click) with an alveolar articulation and lateral release.

Trager and Smith (1951, 45ff) propose an entirely distinct use of the double pipe as a representation of "terminal rise," one of their four juncture phonemes, which is realized by the rising intonation contour typical of English polar (*yes/no*) questions.

COMMENTS

The lateral click consonant referred to is "sometimes used in Western Europe to urge on horses" (Catford 1977, 72). It occurs as a consonant in most Bushman languages and in some Southern Bantu languages, e.g. Zulu (Doke 1926b), and is represented as *x* in the Zulu orthography.

The slash (solidus or oblique stroke) is sometimes found instead of the pipe, giving the transcription '[//]' (q.v.).

SOURCE

Trager (1964, 25) calls this symbol "double bar," but we have dubbed it "double pipe" (the name "pipe" is current among users of the

UNIX computer operating system for the vertical bar symbol) in order to avoid ambiguity about what "bar" means in such names as "barred *i*" or "doubled-barred pipe."

DOUBLE SLASH

IPA USAGE

Not used. The IPA representation for a lateral click is [ʖ].

AMERICAN USAGE

Not standardly used.

OTHER USES

In the South African tradition stemming from 19th century work on the Khoisan languages, often used also by American researchers who have worked on them, represents a velaric ingressive stop (i.e. a click) with an alveolar articulation and lateral release.

COMMENTS

The lateral click consonant referred to is "sometimes used in Western Europe to urge on horses" (Catford 1977, 72). It occurs as a consonant in most Bushman languages and in some Southern Bantu languages, e.g. Zulu (Doke 1926b), and is represented as *x* in the Zulu orthography.

We treat the symbol as an acceptable variant of the double vertical bar symbol ⟨ǁ⟩ (*Double Pipe*, q.v.).

SOURCE

Invented during the 19th century, probably by J. G. Krönlein (see Beach 1938, 288ff).

TRIPLE SLASH

AMERICAN USAGE

Not generally used, but found in Cole (1966, 469) representing a retroflex click (i.e. velaric ingressive retroflex stop).

COMMENTS

The literature on retroflex clicks is complicated and contradictory, but it is clear that genuinely retroflex clicks are extremely rare, and that early work sometimes used the term "retroflex" where it was not justifiable (see Doke 1926b, 128, for an acknowledgment of this). Westerman and Ward (1933, 101) persist in the error, however, using a slash with underdot to represent the alleged retroflex click of Nama (cf. Beach 1938 and Ladefoged and Traill 1984 for closer examination of Nama, and see the entry for [!] above). The IPA definition of [Ɫ] in *Principles* (p. 14) has the error yet again, describing the Zulu *q* click as "retroflex" despite Doke's statement (1926b, 128) that this is an error of earlier work (including his own dissertation), the Zulu *q* being "palato-alveolar." The 1979 IPA chart (Cartier and Todaro 1983) corrects the description by positioning [Ɫ] as post-alveolar but not retroflex.

   Doke (1926a, 148) explicitly describes a retroflex click contrasting with a post-alveolar or palatal click in Ɫhũ:, a Northern Bushman language, which is apparently what Cole is alluding to ("reported for one language, !khũ, of the Northern group"; 1966, 469), but Doke represents them with *ad hoc* symbols of his own devising (see 1926a, 144, for a chart), not with triple slash, which may be idiosyncratic to Cole.

Number Sign

IPA Usage: Not used. *American Usage:* Not a phonetic symbol (except perhaps for Trager); typically found indicating the (grammatically defined) boundaries of a word in phonological representations. Used along with the plus to mark morphological boundaries of various sorts, typically the boundary between words. (Cf. Chomsky and Halle 1968, 12–13.) *Other uses:* In the Trager-Smith (1951, 45ff) analysis of English intonation, used to mark the "terminal fall juncture" phoneme, the falling intonation contour typical of English declarative sentences. *Comments:* The symbol has a variety of names, including crosshatch, double cross, number sign, pound sign, etc.

Asterisk

IPA Usage: Suggested (*Principles,* 17) as a prefix to indicate a word that is a proper name. This recommendation seems to be rarely followed. *American Usage:* No standard use as a phonetic symbol. *Other uses:* Ladefoged (1982, 154–55) suggests the use of the asterisk and an accompanying explanation for any sound that otherwise has no agreed symbol.

Historical linguists use ⟨*⟩ to prefix reconstructed forms—representations of sound properties that do not derive from observation but are rather deduced through historical and comparative reasoning. August Schleicher first used the asterisk in this way.

The most common use of the asterisk among linguists, including phonologists, is as a prefix for ungrammatical or nonexistent forms, sentences, or expressions. This use largely supplants all others in current linguistic practice and is at least as old as Sweet (1898, 3).

Macron

IPA Usage: As a superscript to a vowel symbol, recommended (*Principles,* 18) as a transcription for a high level tone. The IPA suggestion that tone markings be iconic reserves the macron or hyphen as a representation for a level tone, with the pitch to be represented by vertical positioning on the line. Therefore [-ba] would represent a syllable on a mid level tone, [ˉba] or [bā] a high level tone, and [ba] or [ba̯] a low level tone. This iconic use of line position is rare in practice. *American Usage:* Used to mark length or tenseness of a vowel (as in Chomsky and Halle 1968, 51). Also occasionally used in other ways; for example, Mohanan and Mohanan (1984, 598) write [s̄] and [r̄] for palatalized [s] and [r]. Boas et al. (1916, 13) recommend the macron as a diacritic to distinguish a strongly trilled *r* sound from its nontrilled counterpart. The recommendation is not generally followed, but it is perhaps the source of the similar use of the tilde by Pike and Smalley. *Other uses:* Very commonly used for marking vowel length in teaching grammars and in English dictionary pronunciation guides.

Minus Sign

IPA Usage: When not used simply as a hyphen in the ordinary way in broadly transcribed texts, indicates a retracted variety of a vowel or consonant; thus [a−] denotes a vowel somewhat retracted (further back) from Cardinal 4. It can be written [a⊣] if [a−] might be misconstrued as [a] followed by a hyphen. (Cf. *Principles,* 17.) *American Usage:* Reserved by Boas et al. (1916, 8) as a nonphonetic character to be used in indicating the morphological analysis of words in texts.

Under-bar

IPA Usage: Given in *Principles* (p. 17) as a 'retraction sign' to show retracted variants of vowels, or to indicate alveolar place of articulation in a language (e.g. Tamil) that also has dentals. Thus [t̲] is specifically alveolar, leaving [t] to represent the dental stop. Under a vowel symbol or before a symbol, recommended (*Principles,* 18) as a transcription for a low level tone. The IPA suggestion that tone markings be iconic reserves the macron or hyphen as a representation for a level tone, with the pitch to be represented by vertical positioning on the line. Therefore [-ba] would represent a syllable on a mid level tone, [⁻ba] or [bā] a high level tone, and [_ba] or [ba̲] a low level tone. This iconic use of line position is rare in practice. *American Usage:* Unfortunately, sometimes used as a substitute for [ ] to indicate dental place of articulation as opposed to alveolar. Thus Mohanan and Mohanan (1984) use [t] for alveolar and [t̲] for dental in the voiceless stops, the direct converse of the IPA usage. *Other uses:* Pike's *Phonemics* uses underbar to indicate voicelessness; thus Pike's [m̲] is IPA [m̥]. Used as a diacritic in transliterations of Arabic symbols for emphatic (velarized) consonants (cf. Al-Ani 1970, 29). The underdot is also a common diacritic for such transliterations (cf. Beeston 1958, 11). *Comments:* Clearly, caution is in order when the underbar is encountered. It is unfortunate as a diacritic for other reasons as well, notably that a printer's compositor will normally set an underlined character in italic font unless a specific marginal note is attached.

Superscript Equal Sign

Used by Wells (1982, xvii) as a diacritic for unaspirated consonants.

Subscript Bridge

IPA Usage: Under a symbol normally denoting an alveolar consonant, indicates dental place of articulation. Thus [n], [t], [d] etc. are alveolar, and [n̪], [t̪], and [d̪] represent dentals with the same manners of articulation. *American Usage:* Same as IPA, if used, but various substitutes are found. Pike (1947, 7) and Gleason (1955, 7), following Boas et al. (1916, 10), write [t̪] for a voiceless dental stop (IPA [t̪]); Smalley (1963, 454) writes [t̪]; Mohanan and Mohanan (1984, 598), in a recent study of a language with both dental and alveolar consonants, write [t̪].

Plus Sign

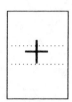

IPA Usage: Indicates an advanced (further front) variety of a vowel or consonant; thus [ɑ+] is a vowel a little further forward than Cardinal 5, and [k+] is a [k] articulated somewhat closer to the palatal area. May also be written as a subscript. Cf. *Principles*, p. 16. *American Usage:* Not generally used as a phonetic character. Boas et al. (1916, 7) recommend its use as an indicator of grammatically insignificant, rhetorical lengthening when transcribing (spoken) texts. *Other uses:* Widely used, along with the number sign ⟨#⟩ and occasionally the equal sign ⟨=⟩ (cf. Aronoff 1976), as an indicator of a morphological boundary. See e.g. Chomsky and Halle (1968, 12–13) where it is used as a formative boundary. Used by Trager and Smith (1951, 38) to mark an "internal open juncture" phoneme that they posit in their analysis of English. The "plus juncture" is the distinguishing element between the pronunciation of English *nitrate* (T&S /náytrèyt/) and *night rate* (T&S /náyt+rèyt/), which are otherwise identical segmentally and suprasegmentally. It is intended to represent a break in the normal articulatory transition between the two consonants across the word boundary in the compound.

Subscript Plus

A subscript plus is used by Smalley (1963, 420) and Samarin (1967, 183) as a diacritic for "breathy" vowels. The IPA's diacritic of advanced articulation can also be written as a subscript.

Raising Sign

IPA Usage: Raising or closing sign: [e˔] indicates a vowel a little higher (closer) than Cardinal 2. Can also be written as a subscript, e.g. [e̞]. The connection between higher and closer gives the use of [w˔] for a voiced labial-velar central fricative in Ladefoged (1968, xviii). Cf. *Principles*, p. 16. *American Usage:* Not used.

Lowering Sign

IPA Usage: Lowering or opening sign: [eτ] indicates a vowel a little lower (more open) than Cardinal 2. Can also be written as a subscript, e.g. [e̞]. The connection between lower and more open gives the use of [ɣτ] for a voiced velar central approximant in Ladefoged (1968, xviii). Cf. *Principles,* p. 16. *American Usage:* Not used.

Vertical Stroke (Superior)

IPA Usage: Indicates primary stress on the following syllable. *Billow* might be transcribed ['bʊloω], and *below* as [bʊ'loω]. *American Usage:* Not entirely standard, but often same as IPA. Boas et al. 1916 recommends the vertical stroke over a vowel symbol as an indicator of mid tone where it is necessary to mark it. *Other uses:* Used by Winston (cf. Welmers 1973, 85) in his transcription of Igbo to mark "downstep," the distinctive lowering of the tonal register within which other tones take their values.

Typographically the character is a vertical stroke of even width. The single quote symbol in most typewriter fonts, which is tapered at the bottom or teardrop shaped, is often used indifferently for this character and the apostrophe (and the reversed apostrophe and the turned comma).

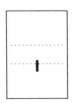

Vertical Stroke (Inferior)

IPA Usage: Indicates a secondary, less prominent stress on the following syllable. *Photographic* might be transcribed [ˌfoʊtəˈgræfɪk].
American Usage: Seldom used.

Syllabicity Mark

IPA Usage: Indicates that the symbol it is written under represents a syllabic sound. *American Usage:* Same as IPA, if used. *Comments:* Not used under symbols for vowels (they are always syllabic) or oral stops, but typically under symbols for liquids or nasals, and occasionally also fricatives. The inverse of ⟨ˌ⟩ is ⟨˘⟩, which is used to indicate the *non*-syllabicity of a vowel.

Corner

IPA Usage: Following a stop consonant symbol, approved (*JIPA* 6, 2) as the official diacritic to represent unreleased stops. Positioned before a syllable, suggested (*Principles,* 18) as a possibility for use in narrow tone transcription for raised or lowered rising tones. *American Usage:* After a stop consonant symbol, used to indicate that the stop is unreleased. Cf. Trager (1964, 26).

Pointers

IPA Usage: Not used. *American Usage:* Used as indicators of altered articulation with vowel symbols and, occasionally, consonant symbols. Cf. Trager (1964, 25–26), Smalley (1963), Pike (1947, 7), Kurath (1939, 129). Their interpretation is iconic: ⌐ is an indicator of backed articulation, ⌐ of fronted, ^ of raised, and ∨ of lowered. Generally used either as right superscripts or (less commonly) right subscripts. For example, Trager writes [k⌐] for a fronted [k], [a⌐] for an advanced [a], etc. *Other uses:.* The raised left arrowhead ⟨⌐⟩ is used by (e.g.) Maddieson (1984) to represent implosives (glottalic ingressive stops); thus [ɢ⌐] = voiced uvular implosive, [p⌐] = voiceless bilabial implosive (see p. 217). Voiceless implosives are very rarely claimed to occur in the literature, and no special unit symbols have been set aside for them.

Superscript Arrow

IPA Usage: Not used. *American Usage:* Used by Smalley (1963, 427) and Samarin (1967, 183) as a diacritic for click (velaric ingressive stop) consonant symbols. Hence [p̄] would be the transcription of a voiceless bilabial unaspirated click.

Over-dot

IPA Usage: According to *Principles* (p. 17), it may be added to a character to denote palatalization. Thus [ż] = [ʑ], [ṡ] = [ɕ], etc. The IPA withdrew approval in 1976 (*JIPA* 6, 3). *American Usage:* Not standard, but may be used as recommended by the IPA. According to the diacritic principles set forth by Boas et al. (1916, 10) the over-dot is used over front and back vowel symbols to create symbols for central vowels. Following this recommendation, Bloch and Trager (1942, 16) and Trager (1964, 22) use [o] to represent a back vowel, [ȯ] a central vowel, and [ö] a front vowel; [e] to represent a front vowel, [ė] a central vowel, and [ë] a back vowel. *Other uses:* Also found as the variant of under-dot (q.v.) used with letters which have descenders (e.g. [ġ] in Trager 1964, 22). *Source:* The convention of writing an over-dot on a consonant that is phonetically palatalized is found in many works on Old English, e.g. Sweet's *Anglo-Saxon Primer.* The Americanist usage is considered a logical extension of the convention for the use of the umlaut diacritic for reversal of backness.

Raised Period

IPA Usage: Strictly speaking, not used (but may be found as a typographical substitution for the half-length mark ⟨ˑ⟩). *American Usage:* Used after a symbol to indicate that the preceding segment is distinctively long. According to the recommendations of Boas et al. (1916, 7), the raised period (⟨·⟩) is the recommended length mark to be used after a symbol to indicate that the sound is long. The colon was designated as marking excessive length, longer than that represented by ⟨·⟩. For languages which make a contrast between only two degrees of length, the colon is generally used as the length mark. Where both indicators occur, the colon represents greater length.

Half-length Mark

IPA Usage: Indicates that "the sound represented by the preceding letter is half-long" (*Principles,* 17). In a narrow transcription of English, the IPA (*Principles,* 20) transcribes *he blew* as [hiˑˈbluː]. *American Usage:* Same as IPA, if used, but a raised period would generally be used instead.

Under-dot

IPA Usage: Indicates a closer (i.e. higher) variety of a vowel; thus IPA [e̞] represents a slightly higher front vowel than IPA [e], as does the alternative notation [e˔] or [e̝]. This use has been extended (*JIPA* 6, 2) to disambiguate the voiced fricative symbols ⟨β⟩, ⟨ð⟩, ⟨z⟩, ⟨ɹ⟩, and ⟨ʁ⟩, which had been officially ambiguous between a fricative and a frictionless approximant. With the under-dot, one of these symbols unambiguously denotes the fricative value. Also extended to [w]. Hence [ẉ] would denote a voiced labiovelar fricative. The corresponding indicator of the approximant value is the subscript half-ring. Thus, the *r*-sounds in English *dread* and *red* may be distinguished as [ɹ̣] and [ɹ] respectively. *American Usage:* Generally, used as a retraction sign for consonants. Thus [x̣] may be found for a backed velar or uvular fricative, [r̄] for a uvular trilled *r*-sound, and so on. Cf. Boas et al. (1916, 10). Retroflex consonants are considered to be retracted alveolars, making the use of the under-dot consistent with the

Indic and Dravidian use described below. The over-dot is sometimes written above letters with descenders (cf. [ġ] in Trager 1964, 22). (The under-dot occurs in the American transcription [ḥ] for a voiceless pharyngeal fricative, IPA [ħ], without its retraction sense.) *Other uses:* Following a tradition established by Sanskritists and commonly used in transliteration of Indic and Dravidian languages, the under-dot under a symbol for an alveolar sound indicates retroflex articulation; thus [ṭ] = IPA [ʈ], etc. Used in Brugmann (1904, 1) as a diacritic for retroflex consonants, and also with *e* and *o* as a diacritic for close vowels. Meillet and Cohen (1952, xiv) use it with the latter sense. Used in some works on African languages to indicate various varieties of vowels. For example [ṳ] may be found for unrounded IPA [ɯ], [ị] may be used for a narrow (retracted tongue-root) variety of high front vowel, and so on (cf. Tucker 1971, Welmers 1973). Also used by Arabists for the "emphatic" consonants, i.e. to denote velarization or pharyngealization (cf. Beeston 1968, 11). *Comments:* The underdot has had too many diverse uses to be used without a note of explanation, and it should be avoided where possible for this reason. The most widely recognized use is probably to represent retroflexion.

Umlaut

IPA Usage: According to *Principles* (p. 16), a diacritic used on a front or back vowel symbol to make a symbol for a central vowel of the same height and rounding as the base vowel: [ï] is an alternative to [ɨ]; [ü] is an alternative to [ʉ]. The diacritic was recommended to indicate that the vowel in question was a member of a back or front vowel phoneme. In 1975, the secretary of the IPA pointed out that "it is widely believed—at least among phoneticians in Britain—that the vowel diacritic [¨] means 'centralized': so that [ë] is between front and central, [ü] between central and back," disagreeing with *Principles.* (He cited Gimson [1970, 38] as an example of this interpretation.) In 1976 the IPA altered the definition of the diacritic [¨] so that it marks a vowel as "centralized," not central (*JIPA* 6, 2). According to this interpretation, [ü] would represent a vowel between [u] and [ʉ]. *American Usage:* Most commonly employed as indicator of reversal of backness of vowels. Suggested in the recommendations of Boas et al. (1916, 9) as a means of extending cardinal vowel signs to create signs for additional vowels. A vowel sign with the umlaut denotes a vowel with the same properties as the base vowel sign with the opposite value for backness. Hence [ï] is a vowel with the same properties as [i] but back instead of front, i.e. IPA [ɯ]; and [ü] is high rounded and front, i.e. IPA [y], and so on. *Comments:* The diacritic of two dots over a vowel symbol is referred to either as the "umlaut" or "dieresis," depending upon the function that it serves. In the orthographies for some European languages (e.g. German) it is used to mark the vowels IPA [y] and [ø] (cf. German *über* 'over', *ölen* 'to oil') which were originally introduced via a vowel fronting sound change called *umlaut*. Functioning as an indicator of dieresis, it is used over the second of two consecutive vowel symbols to indicate that the vowels are to be interpreted as being in separate syllables rather than as a diphthong or else to block the interpretation of the two vowel symbols as a digraph (e.g. English *coöperate, coördinate*). The name *umlaut* has been chosen here because it is generally used to modify vowel symbol denotations in a manner similar to (but much broader than) its use in German orthography.

Subscript Umlaut

IPA Usage: Proposed by Ladefoged (1971, chap. 2) to indicate "breathy voice" or "murmur." Thus [b̤] is a murmured (nearly voiced) stop, [b̤ʱ] is a murmured stop with breathy offglide. The IPA (*JIPA* 6, 2) has adopted this proposal. *American Usage:* Same as IPA, if used. *Other uses:* Used in Meillet and Cohen (1952, xiv) for a diacritic for retroflex consonants.

Colon

IPA Usage: Strictly speaking, not used (but often found as a typographical substitute for the length mark, [ː]). *American Usage:* Marks length of the preceding segment; thus [t:] = [t͡t], [e:] = [e͡e]. According to the recommendations of Boas et al. (1916, 7), the raised period (⟨·⟩) is the recommended length mark to be used after a symbol to indicate that the sound is long. The colon was designated as marking excessive length, longer than that represented by ⟨·⟩. For languages which make a contrast between only two degrees of length, either the colon or the raised period may be used as the length mark. Where both occur, the colon represents greater length. *Comments:* As a punctuation mark, the colon represents something of a pause, so it is a not unnatural choice for indicating increased length.

Length Mark

IPA Usage: Indicates that "the sound represented by the preceding letter is long." Thus [tː] = [t͡t]; [eː] = [e͡e]. *American Usage:* Same as IPA, if used. The colon ⟨:⟩ is generally substituted as a more readily available typographical alternative.

Apostrophe

IPA Usage: Represents "glottal stop simultaneously or almost simultaneously with another sound" (*Principles*, 17). Used as a diacritic to derive symbols for ejective (glottalic egressive) consonants like [p'], [t'], [s'], etc. in Hausa, and also for pulmonic egressive glottal stops in Danish *en* [e'n] and *fem* [fɛm']. *American Usage:* Same as IPA. Recommended by Boas et al. (1916, 14) to represent glottal stop (IPA [ʔ]). Its use was extended as a diacritic for glottalized or ejective consonants, either following the symbol (e.g. [p']) or over the symbol (e.g. ⟨p̍⟩). When used as a diacritic for vowels, it represents laryngealization ("creaky voice"). *Other uses:* Standardly used by Slavicists to indicate palatalization of a preceding consonant. *Comments:* The apostrophe is a raised comma, not the vertical stroke generally found in typewriter fonts. It should be distinct from the (laterally) reversed apostrophe and turned (rotated 180°) comma.

Reversed Apostrophe

IPA Usage: Recommended for weak aspiration after voiceless stops. *JIPA* (6, 2) records the approval of a superscript *h* (ʰ) as an alternative to avoid confusion with the apostrophe diacritic for glottalization. Could be used to distinguish weakly aspirated stops like [pʻ] in English from strongly aspirated stops like [pʰ] in Hindi. *American Usage:* Not in general use, but the use recommended by Boas et al. (1916, 14) is the same as the IPA's: weak aspiration after voiceless stops. *Other uses:* Might be found as a substitute for turned comma as the transliteration of the Arabic character *'ain*, ⟨ ع ⟩, which represents a voiced pharyngeal fricative (IPA [ʕ]). *Comments:* The "rough breathing" of Ancient Greek represented an /h/ onset to a vowel or voiceless onset to an /r/, and looks very similar. This may have influenced the IPA's choice. The distinction between a turned comma and the reversed apostrophe is not observed for reasons of typographical convenience. The reversed apostrophe (the opening single quote in most type fonts) is available as the appropriate rightward facing curl, which makes it useful as a substitution for the rough breathing mark.

 # Turned Comma

IPA Usage: Not used.   *American Usage:* Trager and Smith (1951, 11) use a turned comma as a diacritic for aspiration, rather than the reversed apostrophe.   *Other uses:* Prokosch (1939, 50) uses the turned comma rather than the reversed apostrophe for a diacritic for aspiration. The Arabic character '*ain,* ⟨ ε ⟩, which represents a voiced pharyngeal fricative, IPA [ʕ], is generally transliterated by a turned comma (cf. Beeston 1968, 11), though a reversed apostrophe might be found.   *Comments:* The distinction between a turned comma and the reversed apostrophe is not observed for reasons of typographical convenience. The turned comma (the opening single quote in most type fonts) is available as the appropriate rightward facing curl, which makes it useful as a substitution for the rough breathing mark. On the other hand, the reversed apostrophe cannot be typed, though the turned comma can. Hence, no doubt, the reason for the substitution in Trager and Smith.

Comma

IPA Usage: A punctuation symbol in the usual sense; no phonetic value. *American Usage:* No phonetic value. *Other uses:* Slavicists sometimes use the comma to indicate palatalization of the preceding consonant (much like the IPA's diacritic hook as seen in ⟨ţ⟩); thus Russian [bratʲ] 'to take' might be written ⟨brat,⟩.

Over-ring

IPA Usage: May be used over letters with descenders as an alternative to under-ring (q.v.) to indicate devoicing. Thus *Principles* (p. 16) gives [b̥] and [d̥], but [g̊] rather than [g]. *American Usage:* No standard use. *Other uses:* Abercrombie (1957, 150) and Ladefoged (1982, 51) use a right superscript over-ring to indicate lack of release, e.g. [p°] for unreleased [p]. When the IPA approved the use of the corner symbol ⟨ ⌐⟩ as the accepted diacritic for unreleased stops (*JIPA* 6, 2), the right superscript ring received nearly as many votes. Right superscript over-ring is also used to indicate labialization, e.g. in transcriptions for Caucasian languages (Hewitt 1979 is an example). Also used with the IPA sense by Prokosch (1939, 50). *Source:* The orthographies of the Scandinavian languages use ⟨å⟩ to represent a low back rounded vowel, as in Swedish *skål* 'bowl', suggesting a source for its occasional use as a right superscript to indicate labialization. The over-ring of ⟨ů⟩ in the Czech orthography is called the *kroužek* ('little circle') in Czech. In the various orthographies that employ the over-ring, it has usually originated in a digraph in which an *o* was written above an accompanying vowel.

Under-ring

IPA Usage: "Breath" sign, i.e. devoicing mark. IPA [r̥] is a voiceless trilled *r* (as in certain Scottish dialects in word-final position); [b̥] is a weak (lenis) voiceless bilabial stop (with the slack articulation of a voiced stop but lacking the voicing); [i̥] is a voiceless high front unrounded vowel; and so on. *American Usage:* Generally same as IPA. The under-ring was used as a marker of devoicing in early Americanist work (cf. Boas 1911, 13ff). The recommendations of Boas et al. (1916, 15) substituted the convention for small capital letters for this use and recommended its use as a marker of syllabic consonants. This recommendation was not widely followed and the mark of syllabicity is a short vertical stroke beneath the symbol. *Other uses:* Used by some Indo-Europeanists (e.g. Brugmann 1904, 1; Meillet and Cohen 1952, xiv) as a marker of syllabicity for consonants. Prokosch (1939, 50) uses it in its IPA sense.

Subscript Left Half-ring

IPA Usage: Recommended (*Principles*, 16) to mark open varieties of vowels; thus [e̞] is an alternative to [eʇ] or [e̞]. The IPA (*JIPA* 6, 2) has extended the use of this diacritic to disambiguate the voiced fricative symbols ⟨β⟩, ⟨ð⟩, ⟨z⟩, ⟨ɹ⟩, and ⟨ʁ⟩, which had been officially ambiguous between a fricative and a frictionless approximant. With the subscript left half-ring the symbol unambiguously represents the approximant value. The corresponding indicator of the fricative value is the under-dot. Thus, the *r*-sounds in English *dread* and *red* may be distinguished as [ɹ] and [ɹ̞] respectively. *American Usage:* Found in at least one source (Gleason 1955, 69) marking sounds that start voiceless and become voiced. *Comments:* The diacritic is rarely encountered. Some attempts at the *Polish hook* (q.v.) may look like this when the diacritic is not tied properly to the character body.

Subscript Right Half-ring

IPA Usage: Not used. *American Usage:* Found in Gleason (1955, 69) marking sounds that start voiced and become voiceless. *Comments:* The diacritic is rarely found. Some typographical attempts at a cedilla or a left-hook look like this when not tied properly to the character body.

Superscript Tilde

IPA Usage: Nasalization marker for vowels, or occasionally for consonants; thus [ɑ̃] is a nasalized [ɑ] as in French *en* 'in', [ɣ̃] is a voiced velar fricative articulated with lowered velum, etc. *American Usage:* Various uses. Pike (1947) and Smalley (1963) use it in a number of ways: over ⟨n⟩ for a palatal or palato-alveolar nasal; over other consonants to represent trills ([r̃] alveolar trill; [ʀ̃] uvular trill; [p̃] voiceless bilabial trill: [b̃] voiced bilabial trill); and also over other consonants and vowels to indicate nasalization.

Superimposed Tilde

IPA Usage: Indicates velarization or pharyngealization. (Since these do not contrast in attested languages, there is no ambiguity in practice.) Thus [ɫ] is the velarized "dark" *l*-sound heard in postvocalic position in English; [ḍ] can be used for the arabic "emphatic" *d*-sound; and so on. *American Usage:* Sometimes same as IPA, but some departures are found. For example, [ɫ] may be found for a voiceless alveolar lateral fricative, IPA [ɬ]; and [ƛ] is used for a voiceless alveolar lateral affricate, the tilde being used in place of the crossing bar recommended by Herzog et al. (1934, 631). Halle and Clements (1983, 29) give the superimposed tilde for a "velarized or uvularized" consonant. Most sources do not refer to any such possibility as uvularization (Chomsky and Halle 1968, 307, has the word in a chart but no discussion in the text). Possibly Halle and Clements mean to refer to pharyngealization.

Subscript Tilde

IPA Usage: Not used. Ladefoged's (1982, 302) use of subscript tilde as an indication for creaky voice was proposed to the IPA but acceptance was deferred (*JIPA* 6, 2). *American Usage:* Not standard. Recommended by Smalley (1963, 441) to indicate pharyngealization.

Acute Accent

IPA Usage: Recommended (*Principles*, 18) as a transcription for a high rising tone. The IPA suggestion that tone marking be iconic reserves the acute accent for rising tones, with pitch represented by vertical positioning on the line. Therefore [´ba] (or [bá]) could represent a syllable on a high rising tone, [ˌba] (or [ba̗]) on a low rising tone. The iconic use of line position is rare in practice.   *American Usage:* Generally used either as a tone marker (high tone) or indicator of stress (strongest stress). The recommendations of Boas et al. (1916, 7–8) use the acute accent placed over the vowel sign as an indicator of high tone and as a marker of primary stress when used after the vowel sign. (In languages without tone, the stress may be marked over the vowel.) The Trager-Smith (1951, 37ff) analysis of English stress posits four suprasegmental stress phonemes, marked by ⟨´⟩ (primary), ⟨ˆ⟩ (secondary), ⟨`⟩ (tertiary), and ⟨˘⟩ (weak). The principal contrast in single words is among primary, tertiary, and weak. Trager and Smith's "secondary stress" generally arises as the demotion of the primary stress of a word in a compound. Hence stressed as separate words they give *élevàtor* and *óperàtor,* but stressed as a compound, *élĕvàtŏr ôpĕràtŏr.* The most widely used interpretation of these accents as indicators of stress is: acute, strongest; grave, weaker; breve, weakest.   *Comments:* By extension of the IPA's iconic principles for tone marking, acute accent represents a high (level) tone in register tone languages (e.g. most African tone languages) in contrast to the grave accent for low tone. (Cf. *Practical Orthography for African Languages.*)

Used as an indicator of palatalization (e.g. Brugmann 1904, 1). When written as a right superscript it can be referred to as a prime. It may also be written over a character which has no ascender (e.g. ń, ś, ź in the Polish orthography).

Grave Accent

IPA Usage: Recommended (*Principles,* 18) as a transcription for a high falling tone. The IPA suggestion that tone marking be iconic reserves the grave accent for falling tones, with pitch represented by vertical positioning on the line. Therefore [ˋba] (or [bà]) could represent a syllable on a high falling tone, [ˌba] (or [ba̖]) on a low falling tone. The iconic use of line position is rare in practice. *American Usage:* May vary, but generally used either as a tone marker (low tone) or indicator of stress (nonprimary stress). The recommendations of Boas et al. (1916, 7–8) use the grave accent placed over the vowel sign as an indicator of low tone and as a marker of secondary stress when used after the vowel sign. (In languages without tone, the stress may be marked over the vowel.) The Trager-Smith (1951, 37ff) analysis of English stress posits four suprasegmental stress phonemes, marked ⟨ˊ⟩ (primary), ⟨ˆ⟩ (secondary), ⟨ˋ⟩ (tertiary), and ⟨˘⟩ (weak). The principal contrast in single words is among primary, tertiary, and weak. Trager and Smith's "secondary stress" generally arises as the demotion of the primary stress of a word in a compound. Hence stressed as separate words they give *élĕvàtŏr* and *ópĕràtŏr,* but stressed as a compound, *élĕvàtŏr ôpĕràtŏr.* The most widely used interpretation of these accents as indicators of stress is: acute, strongest; grave, weaker; breve, weakest. *Other uses:* By extension of the IPA's iconic principles for tone marking, grave accent represents a low (level) tone in register tone languages (e.g. most African tone languages) in contrast to the acute accent for high tone. (Cf. *Practical Orthography for African Languages.*)

Circumflex

IPA Usage: Recommended (*Principles,* 18) as a transcription for a rising-falling tone. The IPA suggestion that tone markings be iconic reserves the circumflex for a tone which is a combination of the tones represented by ⟨´⟩ and ⟨`⟩ (in that order). The recommended interpretation of these diacritics as rising and falling tone respectively gives the interpretation of the circumflex as rising-falling. Where the acute and grave accents are interpreted as high and low tones respectively, the circumflex would represent a falling tone. The iconic value as a pointer up apparently explains its use in the IPA example of Yoruba (*Principles,* 45) and Sotho (*Principles,* 49) as a marker of register-rising upstep. *American Usage:* As a tone marking it signifies either rising-falling tone (same as IPA) or falling tone. The Trager-Smith (1951, 37ff) analysis of English stress posits four suprasegmental stress phonemes, marked ⟨´⟩ (primary), ⟨ˆ⟩ (secondary), ⟨`⟩ (tertiary), and ⟨˘⟩ (weak). The principal contrast in single words is among primary, tertiary, and weak. Trager and Smith's "secondary stress" generally arises as the demotion of the primary stress of a word in a compound. Hence stressed as separate words they give *élĕvàtŏr* and *ópèràtŏr,* but stressed as a compound, *élĕvàtŏr ôpĕràtŏr.* *Comments:* The most widely used interpretation of these accents as indicators of stress is: acute, strongest; grave, weaker; breve, weakest. When used as a tone symbol, it probably represents the concatenation of whatever tones the acute and grave accents (respectively) represent. This composition of grave and acute accents to form complex tone symbols is generalized in Goldsmith (1976, 43) where a vowel is marked [ǎ], the result of combining a high tone (´) with a rising tone on [ǎ]. *Source:* Diacritic used over vowels in the orthography of French (e.g. *bête,* 'beast'), but not to mark tone. The circumflex marks vowels which in earlier stages of the language preceded an [s] which has now been lost.

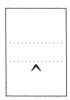

Subscript Circumflex

IPA Usage: Not used. *American Usage:* Used by Smalley (1983, 454) as a fronting diacritic instead of the ⟨ ̯⟩ recommended by Boas et al. (1916, 10). Thus [ṱ] is Smalley's transcription of a voiceless dental stop, [x̭] represents a voiceless palatal fricative (IPA [ç]), and so on.

Wedge

IPA Usage: Recommended (*Principles,* 18) as a transcription for a falling-rising tone. The IPA suggestion that tone markings be iconic reserves the wedge for a tone which is a combination of the tones represented by ⟨`⟩ and ⟨´⟩ (in that order). The recommended interpretation of these diacritics as falling and rising tone respectively gives the interpretation for the wedge as falling-rising. Where the acute and grave are interpreted as high and low tones respectively, the wedge would represent a rising tone. The iconic value as a pointer down apparently explains its use in the IPA example of Igbo, Tswana, and Sotho (*Principles,* 45–49) as a marker of register-lowering downstep. (Welmers [1973, 85] attributes the Igbo example to Ida C. Ward and suggests that it is the earliest valid analysis of a "downstep" tone system.) *American Usage:* Sometimes same as IPA, as a tone symbol. Its principal use is on symbols for alveolar or palatal consonants to represent palato-alveolar fricatives or affricates; thus [š] = IPA [ʃ], [ž] = IPA [ʒ], [č] = IPA [tʃ], [ǰ] = IPA [dʒ]. This use of the hachek or wedge is borrowed from Slavic orthography and explicitly recommended in Herzog et al. (1934, 631). Also used above ⟨r⟩ to indicate certain specific articulation types, e.g. flapped (Smalley 1963, 456–

57) or fricative (Maddieson 1984, 240). *Other uses:* When used as a tone symbol, it probably represents the concatenation of whatever tones the grave and acute accents (respectively) represent. This composition of grave and acute accents to form complex tone symbols is generalized in Goldsmith (1976, 43) where a vowel is marked [ǎ́], the result of combining a high tone (´) with a rising tone on [ǎ]. *Source:* Used in the Czech orthography, where it is called the *haček* ('little hook'), roughly as in the American usage. As a tone mark, it is of course primarily iconic.

Subscript Wedge

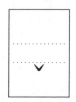

IPA Usage: Indicates that the symbol represents a voiced sound. For example, [s̬] might be used to denote [z] in a language with no [s] ~ [z] contrast but where the *s*-sound was to some extent voiced when between vowels. According to the IPA's conventions for indicating tone, [a̬] could be used for a vowel [a] with a low falling-rising tone, though the iconic use of line position is rare in practice. *American Usage:* Not standardly used.

Polish Hook

IPA Usage: Not used. Not to be confused with the right-hook (q.v.) recommended (*Principles,* 14) for *r*-colored vowels. *American Usage:* Boas et al. (1916, 8) recommend the use of a centered subscript rightward hook under vowel or consonant symbols as a nasalization diacritic. Sometimes used instead of the IPA's tilde diacritic, as by Smalley (1963, 333). Distinct from the IPA diacritic ⟨ç⟩. *Other*

uses: Used to mark nasalized vowels in Polish orthography (letters ę and ą). Used by Brugmann (1904, 1) as a nasalization diacritic for vowels. Used by Meillet and Cohen (1952, xiv) as a diacritic for open vowels, a use similar to the one in historical Germanic studies, which uses it with *e* and *o* as a diacritic for mutated vowels. (Cf. the entries for *E with Polish Hook* and *O with Polish Hook.*)

Cedilla

IPA Usage: Not used as an independent diacritic. *American Usage:* Not used as an independent diacritic. *Other uses:* Used by Brugmann (1904, 1) as an "open vowel" diacritic in contrast to the underdot: [ǫ] is open *o,* [o̩] is close *o;* [ę] is open *e,* [e̩] is close *e.* Note the use of the Rightward Polish hook (e.g. [ę] as a diacritic for mutated vowels in Germanic, cf. Prokosch 1939, 110). Brugmann uses the Polish hook as a nasalization diacritic. *Source:* The cedilla is a diacritic mark on the letter *c* in French orthography.

Palatalization Hook

IPA Usage: Diacritic modification used for constructing symbols for palatalized consonants. An IPA invention; visually reminiscent of ⟨j⟩, which denotes a palatal approximant in the IPA system. *American Usage:* Used to some extent as the IPA uses it, though other ways of showing palatalization are often found (e.g. superscript *y* or *j*). *Comments:* The hook is attached to any convenient lower right part of the basic consonant symbol. The distinctive feature is its leftward turn (by contrast to the rightward turn of the retroflexion diacritic).

For example, Catford (1977, 192) gives the following symbols for Russian palatalized sounds:

Plain	p	b	m	f	v	t	d	n	l	r	s	z
Palatalized	p̡	b̡	m̡	f̡	v̡	t̡	d̡	n̡	l̡	r̡	ˏs	z̡

(We correct Catford's ⟨ʂ⟩ to the IPA's ⟨ʃ⟩. We also change ⟨ɱ⟩ to ⟨m̡⟩, as we suspect a typographical error; ⟨ɱ⟩ has another meaning.)

Right Hook

IPA Usage: Diacritic modification recommended in *Principles* (p. 14) for constructing symbols for vowels with rhotacization (*r*-coloration). Approval for the general use of this diacritic with vowels was withdrawn in 1976 (*JIPA6*, 3) in favor of a digraph such as [aɹ] or [aˑ]. The two symbols [ɚ] and [ɝ] were deemed useful enough to be retained. The IPA's decision to withdraw recognition from this diacritic was prompted by an opinion of the secretary of the IPA, who said of the symbols for rhotacized vowels: "I think no one but Jones ever really liked these symbols, and even he was not enthusiastic" (*JIPA* 5, 1975, 57). But cf. Albright (1958, 61). *American Usage:* Not used. This rightward hook used by the IPA for indicating rhotacization should not be confused with the centered "Polish hook"; for example, [ą] is used in Polish orthography and Americanist (e.g. Smalley's) transcription for nasalized vowels. *Comments:* The similarity to the retroflexion diacritic used by the IPA in [ʂ] and [ʐ] is probably not accidental. This diacritic for retroflexion seems to be latent in certain special symbols for retroflex consonants in the form of a rightward-swept elongation of the rightmost vertical stroke in [ɳ], [ʈ], [ɖ], [ɭ], and [ɽ]. In the interests of terminological consistency, we recognize in this family resemblance an IPA retroflexion indicator, which we call 'right tail'.

Breve

IPA Usage: Used to mark "the weaker element of a diphthong"; thus [ĭu] is like [ju], but [iŭ] is like [iw]. Also used in representing prenasalized stops such as [m̆b], [n̆d], etc. Also suggested (*Principles,* 18) as a possibility for use in narrow tone transcriptions, though no particular interpretation is suggested.   *American Usage:* Sometimes same as IPA; also used to identify specifically unstressed vowels. Recommended by Boas et al. (1916, 7) for use following a symbol to indicate segments which are excessively short. Rare in such use.   *Other uses:* Used to mark short vowels in Classical Latin (in contrast to the macron) as a pedagogical aid. This use gives rise to its occurrence to mark short or lax vowels in the pronunciation guides of some English dictionaries.

Round Cap

IPA Usage: Not used.   *American Usage:* Not used except as a variant of the advancement diacritic ⟨ ̯⟩ (q.v.) with letters which have descenders. Cf. ⟨ĝ⟩ in Trager (1964, 23).   *Other uses:* Used by Brugmann (1904) as a diacritic for palatal stops: [n̂] is the palatal nasal (p. 1). He uses (p. 52) [k̂] and [ĝ] as "palatal" stops and [q] and [g] as true velars, reserving ⟨k⟩ and ⟨g⟩ for cases of uncertainty. (Cf. Prokosch 1939, 42.)

Subscript Arch

IPA Usage: Suggested (*Principles,* 18) as a possibility for use in narrow tone transcriptions (but with no value suggested). *American Usage:* Used by some writers (e.g. Pike [1947, 7] and Gleason [1955, 7]), following Boas et al. (1916, 10), to indicate fronted articulation of a consonant; thus [ŋ̟] may mean a palatal nasal (IPA [ɲ]) and [n̟] may mean a dental nasal (IPA [n̪]). *Other uses:* Used by Brugmann (1904, 1), Wright (1910, 50), and others under a base vowel symbol to denote a semivowel corresponding to the vowel. In their inventory of sounds for Indo-European they provide [u̯] as an alternative to [w], and [i̯] as an alternative to [j]. Used in this sense by Trager and Smith (1951, 11).

Top Ligature

IPA Usage: Synchronic articulation sign: [ŋ͡m] is a labiovelar nasal; [ɔ͡ɪ] could represent an *r*-colored schwa (same as [ɚ]); [a͡ɪ] represents a diphthong composed of [a] and [ɪ]; and so on. *American Usage:* Same as IPA, if used. *Comments:* The bottom ligature is used for the same purpose with characters which do not have descenders. The "close-up" notation *a͡z* as an editor's mark in proof correction indicates that the two characters should be brought together. Trager and Smith (1951, 37) call it the "tie line."

Bottom Ligature

IPA Usage: Synchronic articulation sign: [b͜d] would indicate a simultaneously bilabial and alveolar stop; [ə͜ɹ] could represent an *r*-colored schwa (same as [ɚ]); [a͜ʊ] represents a diphthong composed of [a] and [ʊ]; and so on. *American Usage:* Same as IPA, if used. *Comments:* The top ligature is used for the same purpose with characters which have descenders. The "close-up" notation *a͡z* as an editor's mark in proof correction indicates that the two characters should be brought together. Trager and Smith (1951, 37) call it the "tie line."

GLOSSARY

This glossary is not a complete dictionary of phonetic terminology, but it gives basic definitions for the technical terms used in this book, and explains equivalences between terms used in quotations from authors that we cite.

Advanced.   Articulated with a tongue position closer to the front of the mouth (relative to some given position).

Affricate.   Consonant composed of an initial stop phase followed by a release phase taking the form of a homorganic fricative.

Alveolar.   Relating to the alveolar ridge, the bony ridge behind the upper teeth.

Alveolo-palatal.   Relating to the region just behind the palato-alveolar, but further forward than the palatal. (This term is now not much used. For a chart that clarifies its rather limited domain, see p. 262.)

Alveopalatal.   Relating to the region between the alveolar ridge and the (hard) palate. (A term used in many American texts, e.g. Smalley 1963, Gleason 1955, covering both the palato-alveolar and alveolo-palatal regions of the IPA system.)

Apical.   Relating to the apex (tip) of the tongue.

Approximant.   Frictionless continuant. For Ladefoged, who coined the term (1964), a consonantal sound articulated in a manner involving an opening in the oral tract not radical enough to produce audible friction; thus, IPA [j], [w], [l], etc. Catford (1977, 119–22) refines this, defining approximants as having non-turbulent airflow when voiced but turbulent airflow when voiceless.

Articulator.   A delimited part of the vocal tract that plays a specific role in the production of a speech sound; thus, articulators include the lips, teeth, tongue-tip, hard palate, uvula, etc.

Arytenoid A pair of cartilages on top of the larynx, attached to the back of the vocal cords and capable of separating them (as in the production of voiceless sounds) and partially or completely bringing them together.

Aspirated. Immediately followed by a brief delay in onset of normal voicing state. Used of pulmonic stop consonants, particularly voiceless ones, e.g. English [pʰ] in [pʰɛt] 'pet'.

Back. (Of vowels) Articulated with the highest point of the tongue at the back of the mouth, i.e. below the soft palate.

Bilabial. Relating to articulation involving the two lips.

Breathy voice. Murmur; articulation with heavy airflow through the slightly open glottis and some vibration of the vocal cords, but not as much as in full voicing.

Cacuminal. An older synonym for retroflex.

Cardinal. (Of vowels) Relating to the system of Cardinal Vowels devised by Daniel Jones for representing vowel quality in terms of a grid of absolute values. Cardinal ı is defined as the highest and most front vowel physiologically producible; Cardinal 5 is defined as the lowest and most back vowel physiologically producible; Cardinals ı, 2, 3, and 4 are front unrounded vowels whose openness evenly increases toward the maximum possible, and Cardinals 5, 6, 7, and 8 are back vowels whose closeness and rounding evenly increases toward the maximum possible. A second series, Cardinals 9 through 16, is then defined as having identical tongue positions but opposite rounding. (Cf. the charts on pp. 000–000.)

Central. (Of consonants) Non-lateral, i.e. articulated in a manner that involves airflow predominantly down the center line of the oral cavity (from uvula to middle front teeth) rather than around the sides of the tongue; (of vowels) involving a tongue position with its highest point neither in the front third nor in the back third of the oral cavity, i.e. roughly below the junction of the hard and soft palates. Note that for consonants the center referenced is between left and right cheeks, but for vowels the center is between front and back of the oral cavity. *Median* is an unambiguous and thus preferable term for the former.

Centralized. (Of vowels) Articulated with the highest tongue position somewhat closer to the center (between front and back) than is normal for the vowel type in question; that is, for a front vowel, somewhat retracted, and for a back vowel, somewhat advanced. (A central vowel, clearly, cannot be centralized.)

Cerebral. An older synonym for retroflex.

Click. Stop consonant formed with a velaric ingressive airstream, i.e., with inflowing release of air triggered by release of a stop closure in the forward part of the oral tract, using suction developed by downward movement of the tongue body while maintaining a dorso-velar closure.

Close. (Of vowels) High; with tongue position close to the roof of the mouth; the opposite of open.

Coarticulated. Articulated in a manner simultaneously involving two (or more) distinct areas of the vocal tract. This may mean two or more articulatory gestures of a similar sort at different locations (e.g., dorso-velar stop closure together with bilabial closure in a labial-velar stop such as [kp]) or superimposition of a less radical articulatory gesture on a more radical one (as with labialization of a velar stop such as [kʷ]).

Creaky voice. Laryngealization; articulation with the back end of the vocal cords held together by the arytenoid cartilages so that only the other end can vibrate.

Dental. Relating to the upper front teeth.

Diphthong. Sequence of two perceptibly different vowel sounds (or a vowel sound and a glide) in the same syllable.

Dorsal. Relating to the dorsum, the back third of the tongue.

Egressive. (Of airstreams) Going outward.

Ejective. Glottalic egressive consonant.

Emphatic. A term traditionally used to describe the pharyngealized series of consonants in Arabic.

Flap. Consonant articulated in a manner that involves one articulator being retracted and then striking another in passing during the trajectory of its return to its rest position.

Flat. (Articulatory) Not grooved. (Not the same as the acoustic sense of this term, which refers to the property of displaying a general downward shifting of formant structure.)

Fortis. Articulated in a manner involving more energetic tensing of the articulatory musculature; opposite of lenis.

Fricative. Consonantal sound articulated in a manner involving approximation of articulators to narrow a part of the oral tract radically enough to produce audible friction.

Front. (Of vowels) Articulated with the highest point of the tongue in the front region of the mouth, i.e. below the hard palate.

Glide. Nonvocalic central approximant; semivowel.

Glottal. Relating to the glottis or to the vocal cords.

Glottalic. Relating to a mode of creating oral airflow in the pharynx by raising or lowering the larynx with glottis closed. (Lowering the larynx can create implosive stops; raising the larynx can create ejectives.)

Glottis. The space between the vocal cords through which air passes during production of pulmonic egressive sounds.

Grooved. Articulated with a slight concavity of the upper surface of the tongue in proximity to the alveolar or palato-alveolar region, forming a groove through which air passes with strong friction.

Guttural. According to Prokosch (1939, 42): "This somewhat inept term is generally used in comparative grammars to designate consonants that are articulated either against the hard or the soft palate, and it may well serve as a collective term of expedience." Obsolete.

Half-close. (Of vowels) Articulated with a tongue height between mid and close.

Half-open. (Of vowels) Articulated with a tongue height between mid and open.

High. (Of vowels) Articulated with a tongue height that involves raising the body of the tongue above its neutral position to (or near) the maximal extent possible; (fully) close.

Higher-mid. (Of vowels) Articulated with a tongue height slightly higher than the mid position; at or around the height of Cardinal 2.

Higher-low. (Of vowels) Articulated with a tongue height slightly higher than the maximally low position; between the height of Cardinal 3 and Cardinal 4.

Homorganic. Having the same place of articulation (as some given adjacent segment, for example).

Implosive. Stop consonant formed with a glottalic ingressive airstream, that is, with inflowing release of air using suction developed by downward movement of the larynx while another complete obstruction is maintained further forward in the oral tract.

Ingressive.   (Of airstreams) Moving inward.

Interdental.   Relating to the gap between the upper and lower front teeth.

Labial.   Involving use of or contact with the lips.

Labialized.   Articulated in a manner that secondarily involves the rounding of the lips.

Labiodental.   Articulated by bringing the lower lip into contact with the upper teeth.

Labial-velar, Labiovelar.   Relating to an articulation involving both the lips (either rounded or closed) and the dorsal part of the tongue raised toward the velum.

Laminal.   Relating to the blade of the tongue (the middle third), as opposed to the tip or the back.

Laryngal, Laryngeal.   Relating to the larynx.

Laryngealized.   Articulated with creaky voice, i.e. with the back end of the vocal cords held together by the arytenoid cartilages so that only the other end can vibrate.

Lateral.   Articulated in a manner that involves oral airflow predominantly around a central obstruction across the sides of the tongue rather than down the center line of the oral cavity.

Lax.   The opposite of tense.

Lenis.   Articulated in a manner involving laxer operation of the articulatory musculature; antonym of fortis.

Liquid.   A term used for the general category comprising the lateral sonorants and (most varieties of) *r*-sounds.

Low.   (Of vowels) Articulated in a manner that involves lowering the tongue below its neutral position to (or near) the maximal extent possible; (fully) open.

Lower-high.   (Of vowels) Articulated with the highest point of the tongue slightly lower than the maximally high position; between the height of Cardinal 1 and Cardinal 2.

Lower-mid.   (Of vowels) Articulated with the highest point of the tongue slightly lower than the mid position; at or around the height of Cardinal 3.

Mean-mid.   (Of vowels) Articulated with the highest point of the tongue at the mean (average) of the mid region; between the higher-mid (Cardinal 2) and lower-mid (Cardinal 3) positions. A term used in Bloch and Trager (1943).

Median. (Of consonants) Central, i.e. articulated in a manner that involves airflow predominantly down the center line of the oral cavity (from uvula to middle front teeth) rather than around the sides of the tongue. The word *central* refers ambiguously to a non-lateral consonant or to a vowel between front and back, hence *median* is preferable for the former.

Mid. (Of vowels) Articulated with the highest point of the tongue at its neutral position, half way between fully open (low) and fully close (high); between the heights of Cardinal 2 and Cardinal 3.

Murmur. Breathy voice.

Nasal. Stop consonant articulated with a lowered velum, produced by airflow through the nasal cavity rather than the oral cavity. (As an adjective, it is synonymous with *nasalized*.)

Nasalized. Articulated with the velum lowered so that airflow is permitted through the nasal cavity as well as through the oral cavity.

Obstruent. Non-resonant consonant, i.e. specifically a stop, fricative, or affricate.

Open. (Of vowels) Low; with the jaw relatively open and the highest part of the tongue far from the roof of the mouth.

Oral. Articulated with the velum raised so that airflow is permitted solely through the oral cavity, not the nasal cavity.

Palatal. Relating to the hard palate or roof of the oral cavity.

Palatalized. Articulated in a manner that involves a secondary articulatory gesture of raising the blade of the tongue toward the hard palate.

Palate. The roof of the mouth. The hard palate is the bony central region of the roof of the mouth; the soft palate or velum is the soft flap of tissue between it and the uvula.

Palato-alveolar. Relating to the region just behind the alveolar ridge. (The IPA draws a distinction between the palato-alveolar region, roughly where the English consonant in *shy* is articulated, and the alveolo-palatal region, which is slightly further back, but still not palatal; see *Principles*, p. 10.)

Peripheral. (Of vowels) Involving a tongue position with its highest point in either the front or the back of the oral cavity; not central.

Pharyngal, Pharyngeal. Relating to or involving the pharynx.

Pharyngealized. Articulated in a manner which secondarily involves constriction of the pharynx by retraction of the root of the tongue.

Plosive. Pulmonic egressive stop consonant.

Postvelar. Relating to the region immediately behind the velum; as a position of articulation for consonants, effectively equivalent to uvular.

Pulmonic. Relating to a mode of creating airflow in the vocal tract by the use of the respiratory muscles.

Raised. Articulated with a higher tongue position.

Resonant. Consonant articulated in a manner in which either the oral or the nasal passage is relatively free of obstruction. In other words, a non-obstruent. Covers the glides, nasals, laterals, and (most varieties of) *r*-sounds.

Retracted. Articulated with a tongue position closer to the back of the mouth (relative to some given position).

Retroflex. Articulated in a manner involving retraction of the apex of the tongue so that its lower surface is brought into proximity to the hard palate.

Retroflexed. Rhotacized.

Rhotacized. *R*-colored; produced with a secondary articulatory gesture involving tongue positioning similar to that employed for *r*-sounds (especially the retroflex glide *r*-sound).

Rounded. Articulated in a manner that involves rounding of the lips.

Secondary. Modifying articulatory gesture, usually involving less radical constriction of the vocal tract than another simultaneous one; thus, e.g., labialization of a velar stop as in [kʷ]. See Catford (1977, 188ff) for a more careful definition.

Semivowel. Nonvocalic central approximant; glide.

Shibilant. A term occasionally found for a fricative corresponding to a "hushing" sound, e.g. IPA [ʃ] (more technically, a grooved laminal fricative). Not a standard term.

Sibilant. An older term for a fricative corresponding to a "hissing sound," e.g. [s]; more technically, a grooved apical fricative.

Sonant. An older term for a voiced sound. Obsolete.

Sonorant. Consonant articulated in a manner in which either the oral or the nasal passage is relatively free of obstruction. In other words, a non-obstruent. Covers the glides, nasals, laterals, and (most varieties of) *r*-sounds.

Spirant. An older term for a fricative. Almost obsolete.

Spirantization. A change from a stop articulation to a spirant (fricative) one by sound change or by phonological rule.

Spread. (Of vowels) The opposite of rounded; another term for unrounded.

Stop. Consonant articulated in a manner involving a complete blockage of airflow somewhere in the oral tract.

Strangulated. A term found in Boas et al. (1916), apparently meaning "articulated with constriction of the pharynx." Not accepted phonetic terminology.

Surd. An older term for voiceless sound. Obsolete.

Tap. Consonant formed in a manner that involves a mobile active articulator (typically the apex of the tongue) tapping once very rapidly on a passive articulator (e.g. the alveolar ridge).

Tense. A problematic term phonetically; it is claimed by some that there is an identifiable class of tense speech sounds characterized by an articulation involving relatively more forceful and extreme motions of the articulators, but there is considerable controversy in the experimental literature about such phonetic correlates. In phonology, the feature has played an important role in Chomsky and Halle's (1968) classification of the English vowels, the long vowels and diphthongs being called tense and the short vowels lax.

Trill. Consonant articulated in a manner that involves a mobile active articulator fluttering in a turbulent air stream and striking another articulator rapidly and repeatedly—for example, the apex of the tongue fluttering against the alveolar ridge, or the uvula vibrating against the root of the tongue.

Upper. (Of vowels) Articulated with the highest point of the tongue between the mid position and the high position; at or around the height of Cardinal 2.

Uvula. The small appendage of soft tissue hanging down at the back of the mouth, at the lower end of the velum.

Uvular. Relating to the uvula.

Velar. Relating to the velum.

Velaric. Relating to a mode of creating oral airflow by movement of a closure formed by the dorsal region of the tongue against the velum.

Velarized. Articulated in a manner which secondarily involves raising the tongue toward the velum.

Velum. The movable fold of tissue at the back of the roof of the mouth, commonly known as the soft palate.

Voiced. Articulated in a manner involving free vibration of the vocal cords under influence of pulmonic airflow through the larynx and glottis.

Voiceless. Articulated in a manner not involving free vibration of the vocal cords under influence of pulmonic airflow through the larynx and glottis.

REFERENCES

Abercrombie, David. 1967. *Elements of General Phonetics*. Edinburgh: Edinburgh University Press.

Al-Ani, Salman H. 1970. *Arabic Phonology*. The Hague: Mouton.

Albright, Robert William. 1958. The International Phonetic Alphabet: Its backgrounds and development. *International Journal of American Linguistics* 24 (January). Indiana University, Research Center in Anthropology, Folklore and Linguistics, Publication 7. Bloomington.

Arnott, D. W. 1964. Downstep in the Tiv Verbal System. *African Language Studies* 5: 34–51.

Aronoff, Mark. 1976. *Word Formation in Generative Grammar*. Cambridge: MIT Press.

Bach, Emmon, and Robert T. Harms, eds. 1968. *Universals in Linguistic Theory*. New York: Holt, Rinehart and Winston.

Bailey, T. Grahame. 1956. *Teach Yourself Urdu*. Edited and revised by J. R. Firth and A. H. Harley. London: The English Universities Press.

Beach, D. M. 1938. *The Phonetics of the Hottentot Language*. Cambridge: Heffer.

Beeston, A. F. L. 1968. *Written Arabic*. Cambridge: Cambridge University Press.

Bleek, D. F. 1926. Note on Bushman orthography. *Bantu Studies* 2 (1923–1926), 71–74.

Bloch, Bernard, and George L. Trager. 1942. *Outline of Linguistic Analysis*. Baltimore: Linguistic Society of America.

Bloomfield, Leonard. 1933. *Language*. New York: Holt, Rinehart and Winston.

Boas, Franz. 1911. *Handbook of American Indian Languages,* part 1.

Smithsonian Institution Bureau of American Ethnology, Bulletin 40. Washington, D.C.: Government Printing Office.

Boas, Franz, P. E. Goddard, Edward Sapir, and A. L. Kroeber. 1916. *Phonetic Transcription of American Indian Languages: Report of Committee of American Anthropological Association.* Smithsonian Institution, Publication 2415 (September). Also in Smithsonian Miscellaneous Collections 66 (1917), publication no. 2478, item no. 6. Washington: Smithsonian Institution.

Boas, Franz, and John R. Swanton. 1911. Siouan: Dakota (Teton and Santee dialects) with remarks on the Ponca and Winnebago. In Boas (1911), 875–965.

Brauner, Wilhelm. 1967. *Althochdeutsche Grammatik.* Edited by Walther Mitzka. Tübingen: Max Niemeyer. Reader. New York: Henry Holt and Co.

Bright, James W. 1935. *Bright's Anglo-Saxon Reader.* 1959 reprint. Revised and enlarged by James R. Hulbert. New York: Henry Holt and Co.

Brugmann, Karl. 1904. *Kurze Vergleichende Grammatik der Indogermanischen Sprachen.* Strassburg: Karl J. Trübner.

Bush, Clara, et al. 1973. On specifying a system for transcribing consonants in child language: A working paper with examples from American English and Mexican Spanish. Unpublished paper, Child Language Project, Stanford University, CA.

Caffee, N. M. 1940. Southern 'l' plus a consonant. *American Speech* 15:259–61.

Carmody, Francis J. 1945. *Is* in Modern Scottish Gaelic. *Word* 1:162–87.

Cartier, Francis A., and Martin T. Todaro. 1971. *The Phonetic Alphabet.* 3d ed. Dubuque, Iowa: Wm. C. Brown.

Catford, J. C. 1977. *Fundamental Problems in Phonetics.* Bloomington: Indiana University Press.

Chao, Yuen-Ren. 1934. The non-uniqueness of phonemic solutions of phonetic systems. *Bulletin of the Institute of History and Philology, Academia Sinica,* vol. 4, part 4:363–97. Page references to the reprint in Joos (ed.): 38–54.

Chicago Manual of Style. 1982. 13th ed., rev. and exp. Chicago: University of Chicago Press.

Chistovich, L. A., et al. 1982. Temporal processing of peripheral auditory patterns of speech. *The Representation of Speech in the Peripheral Auditory System,* ed. Rolf Carlson and Björn Granström, 165–80. New York: Elsevier Biomedical Press.

Chomsky, Noam. 1964. Current issues in linguistic theory. In Fodor and Katz (1964), 50–118.

Chomsky, Noam, and Morris Halle. 1968. *The Sound Pattern of English.* New York: Harper and Row.

Cole, Desmond T. 1966. Bushman languages. *Encyclopedia Britannica,* vol. 4, 468–70.

Crothers, John. 1978. Typology and universals of vowel systems. In *Universals of Human Language.* Volume 2: *Phonology,* ed. Joseph H. Greenberg, 93–152. Stanford: Stanford University Press.

Danesi, Marcel. 1982. The description of Spanish /b, d, g/ revisited. *Hispania* 65:252–58.

Dinnsen, Daniel A. 1974. Constraints on global rules in phonology. *Language* 50:29–51.

Doke, Clement M. 1926a. An outline of the phonetics of the language of the ɕhũ: Bushmen of North-West Kalahari. *Bantu Studies* 2 (1923–26):129–65.

———. 1926b. *The Phonetics of the Zulu Language.* Bantu Studies Supplement. Johannesberg: University of the Witwatersrand Press. Repr. Nendeln/Lichtenstein: Kraus, 1969.

Ellis, Jeffrey. 1953. *An Elementary Old High German Grammar, Descriptive and Comparative.* Oxford: Clarendon Press.

Fairbanks, Gordon H., and Bal Govind Misra. 1966. *Spoken and Written Hindi.* Ithaca, NY: Cornell University Press.

Firth, J. R. 1948. Sounds and prosodies. *Transactions of the Philological Society,* 127–52. Reprinted in Firth (1957:121–38), and in Jones and Laver (1973:47–65); photoreproduced from the original source in Palmer (1970:1–26). Page references to the original.

———. 1957. *Papers in Linguistics 1934–1951.* London: Oxford University Press.

Fodor, Jerry A., and Jerrold J. Katz, eds. 1964. *The Structure of Language: Readings in the Philosophy of Language.* Englewood Cliffs, NJ: Prentice-Hall.

Fontanals, Joaquín Rafel. 1976. Areas léxicas en una encrucijada lingüística. *Revista de filología española* 5 (1974–75):231–75.

Gimson, A. C. 1962. *An Introduction to the Pronunciation of En-*

glish. 1st ed. London: Edward Arnold. 2d ed., 1970. 3d ed., 1980.

Gleason, Henry Allan. 1955. *Workbook in Descriptive Linguistics.* New York: Holt, Rinehart and Winston.

Goldsmith, John. 1976. An overview of autosegmental phonology. *Linguistic Analysis* 2:23–68.

Greenberg, Joseph H., ed. 1978. *Universals of Human Language.* Volume 2: *Phonology.* Stanford: Stanford University Press.

Gruber, Jeffrey S. 1973. ǂHõã kinship terms. *Linguistic Inquiry* 4:427–49.

Grunwell, Pam, et al. 1980. The phonetic representation of disordered speech. *British Journal of Disorders of Communication* 15:215–20.

Halle, Morris, and G. N. Clements. 1983. *Problem Book in Phonology.* Cambridge: MIT Press.

Halle, Morris, and K. P. Mohanan. 1985. The segmental phonology of modern English. *Linguistic Inquiry* 16:57–116.

Hamp, Eric P. 1951. Morphophonemes of the Keltic mutations. *Language* 27:230–47.

———1965a. Evidence in Albanian. In Winter (1965), 123–41.

———1965b. Evidence in Keltic. In Winter (1965), 224–35.

Hamp, Eric P., Fred W. Householder, and Robert Austerlitz, eds. 1966. *Readings in Linguistics II.* Chicago: University of Chicago Press.

Harley, A. H. 1944. *Colloquial Hindustani.* London: Kegan Paul, Trench, Trubner and Co. Ltd.

Herzog, George, Stanley S. Newman, Edward Sapir, Mary Haas, Morris Swadesh, and Charles F. Voegelin. 1934. Some orthographic recommendations. *American Anthropologist,* n.s., 36:629–31.

Hewitt, B. G., in collaboration with Z. K. Khiba. 1979. *Abkhaz. Lingua Descriptive Studies* 2. Amsterdam: North-Holland.

Hockett, Charles F. 1955. *A Manual of Phonology.* IJAL Memoir 11. International Journal of American Linguistics 21, no. 4, part 1. Chicago: University of Chicago Press.

Hoffmann, C. F. 1963. *A Grammar of the Margi Language.* Oxford: Oxford University Press.

Hoijer, Harry. 1945. *Navaho Phonology.* University of New Mexico

Publications in Anthropology, no. 1. Albuquerque: University of New Mexico Press.

Hughes, Arthur, and Peter Trudgill. 1979. *English Accents and Dialects.* London: Edward Arnold.

Hyman, Larry. 1975. *Phonology: Theory and Analysis.* New York: Holt, Rinehart and Winston.

Ingram, David. 1976. *Phonological Disability in Children.* London: Edward Arnold.

International African Institute. 1930. *Practical Orthography of African Languages.* International African Institute, Memorandum 1. Oxford: Oxford University Press.

International Phonetic Association. 1949 (repr. 1967). *The Principles of the International Phonetic Association.* London: Dept. of Phonetics, University College (now Dept. of Phonetics and Linguistics, University College London).

Jespersen, Otto. 1949. *A Modern English Grammar on Historical Principles.* Part 1, *Sounds and Spellings.* Copenhagen: Einar Munksgaard; London: George Allen and Unwin.

———. 1962. *Growth and Structure of the English Language.* 9th ed. Oxford: Basil Blackwell.

JIPA: Journal of the International Phonetic Association (formerly *Le Maître Phonétique*). London: International Phonetic Association.

Jones, Charles. 1972. *An Introduction to Middle English.* New York: Holt, Rinehart and Winston.

Jones, Daniel. 1918. *An Outline of English Phonetics.* 1st ed. Cambridge: W. Heffer and Sons.

———. 1956. *The Pronunciation of English.* 4th ed. Cambridge: Cambridge University Press.

———. 1957. *The History and Meaning of the Term 'Phoneme'.* First published as a supplement to *Le Maître Phonétique,* and issued as a pamphlet by the International Phonetic Association (University College London). Reprinted as an appendix to Daniel Jones, *The Phoneme,* 3d ed. (Cambridge: Heffer, 1967), 253–69. Reprinted in Jones and Laver (1973), 187–204.

———. 1962. *An Outline of English Phonetics.* 9th ed. Cambridge: W. Heffer and Sons.

Jones, W. E. and J. Laver, eds. 1973. *Phonetics in Linguistics: A Book of Readings.* London: Longman.

Jones, William. 1911. Algonquian (Fox). (Revised by Truman Michelson.) Boas 1911: 735–873.

Joos, Martin, ed. 1966. *Readings in Linguistics I*. 4th ed. Chicago: University of Chicago Press.

Kaufman, Terrence. 1970. *Proyecto de alfabetos y ortografías para escribir las lenguas mayances*. Antigua, Guatemala: Proyecto Lingüístico Francisco Marroquín.

Kenyon, John Samuel. 1950. *American Pronunciation*. 10th ed. Ann Arbor, MI: George Wahr.

Kiparsky, Paul. 1968. Linguistic universals and linguistic change. In *Universals in Linguistic Theory*, ed. Emmon Bach and Robert T. Harms, 170–202. New York: Holt, Rinehart and Winston.

Kurath, Hans. 1939. *Handbook of the Linguistic Geography of New England*. Providence, RI: Brown University.

Kurath, Hans, and Raven McDavid, Jr. 1961. *The Pronunciation of English in the Atlantic States*. Studies in American English, 3. Ann Arbor: University of Michigan Press.

Ladefoged, Peter. 1968. *A Phonetic Study of West African Languages*. Chicago: University of Chicago Press.

———. 1971. *Preliminaries to Linguistic Phonetics*. Chicago: University of Chicago Press.

———. 1982. *A Course in Phonetics*. 2d ed. New York: Harcourt Brace Jovanovich.

Ladefoged, Peter, and Anthony Traill. 1984. Linguistic phonetic description of clicks. *Language* 60: 1–20.

Lepsius, Richard. 1863. *Standard Alphabet for Reducing Unwritten Languages and Foreign Graphic Systems to a Uniform Orthography in European Letters*, Ed. J. Alan Kemp; Amsterdam Studies in the Theory and History of Science, 5. Amsterdam: John Benjamins, 1981.

McCloskey, James. 1979. *Transformational Syntax and Model-Theoretic Semantics*. Dordrecht: D. Reidel.

Maddieson, Ian. 1984. *Patterns of Sounds*. Cambridge: Cambridge University Press.

Meillet, A., and Marcel Cohen. 1952. *Les Langues du Monde*. Paris: C.N.R.S.

Mohanan, K. P., and Tara Mohanan. 1984. Lexical phonology of the consonant system in Malayalam. *Linguistic Inquiry* 15: 575–602.

Monzón, Cristina, and Andrew Roth Seneff. 1984. Notes on the Nahuatl phonological change $k^w \rightarrow b$. *IJAL* 50:456–62.

Moore, Samuel, and Thomas A. Knott. 1955. *The Elements of Old English*. 10th ed. Revised by James R. Hulbert. Ann Arbor, MI: George Wahr Publishing Co.

Palmer, F. R., ed. 1970. *Prosodic Analysis*. London: Oxford University Press.

Pike, Kenneth L. 1943. *Phonetics*. Ann Arbor: University of Michigan Press.

————. 1947. *Phonemics: A Technique for Reducing Languages to Writing*. Ann Arbor: University of Michigan Press.

Pitman, James, and John St. John. 1969. *Alphabets and Reading*. New York: Pitman Publishing.

Polomé, Edgar. 1965. The laryngeal theory so far. In Winter (1965), 9–78.

Postal, Paul M. 1964. Limitations of phrase structure grammars. In Fodor and Katz (1964), 137–51.

Prokosch, E. 1939. *A Comparative Germanic Grammar*. Philadelphia: Linguistic Society of America, University of Pennsylvania.

Quilis, Antonio, and María Vaquero. 1974. Realizaciones de /c/ en el área metropolitana de San Juan de Puerto Rico. *Revista de filología española* 56 (1973): 1–52.

Quirk, Randolph, and C. L. Wrenn. 1957. *An Old English Grammar*. London: Methuen; New York: Holt, Rinehart and Winston.

Samarin, William J. 1967. *Field Linguistics*. New York: Holt, Rinehart and Winston.

Sapir, Edward. 1925. Sound patterns in language. *Language* 1: 37–51.

Smalley, William A. 1963. *Manual of Articulatory Phonetics*. Rev. ed. Tarrytown, NY: Practical Anthropology.

Spier, Leslie. 1946. *Comparative Vocabularies and Parallel Texts in Two Yuman Languages of Arizona*. Univ. of New Mexico Publications in Anthropology, 2. Albuquerque: University of New Mexico Press.

Suarez, Jorge A. 1983. *The Mesoamerican Indian Languages*. Cambridge: Cambridge University Press.

Sweet, Henry. 1877. *A Handbook of Phonetics*. Oxford: Henry Frowde.

————. 1882. *Sweet's Anglo-Saxon Primer.* Revised by Norman Davis. Oxford: Clarendon Press.

————. 1891. *A New English Grammar, Logical and Historical. Part 1, Introduction, Phonology, and Accidence.* Oxford: Clarendon Press.

————. 1898. *A New English Grammar, Logical and Historical. Part 2, Syntax.* Oxford: Clarendon Press.

Thalbitzer, William. 1911. Eskimo. In Boas (1911), 967–1069.

Trager, George L. 1964. *Phonetics: Glossary and Tables.* 2d ed., rev. (*Studies in Linguistics: Occasional Papers* 6.) Buffalo, NY: George L. Trager.

Trager, George L., and Henry Lee Smith, Jr. 1951. *An Outline of English Structure.* (*Studies in Linguistics: Occasional Papers* 3.) Norman, Oklahoma: Battenburg Press. Page references to 6th printing, American Council of Learned Societies, Washington D.C., 1965.

Trubetzkoy, N. S. 1932. Das mordwinische phonologische System verglichen mit dem Russischen. *Charisteria V. Mathesio oblata,* 21–24. Prague: Cercle Linguistique de Prague. Page references to the reprint in Hamp et al. (1966), 38–41.

————. 1969. *Principles of phonology.* Translated by Christiane A. M. Baltaxe. Berkeley: University of California Press.

Tucker, A. N. 1971. Orthographic systems and conventions in Sub-Saharan Africa. In *Linguistics in Sub-Saharan Africa,* ed. Jack Berry and Joseph H. Greenberg, 618–53. Current Trends in Linguistics 7. The Hague: Mouton.

Wells, J. C. 1982. *Accents of English I.* Cambridge: Cambridge University Press.

Welmers, William E. 1973. *African Language Structures.* Berkeley: University of California Press.

Westerman, D., and Ida C. Ward. 1933. *Practical Phonetics for Students of African Languages.* London: Oxford University Press.

Westphal, E. O. J. 1971. The click languages of Southern and Eastern Africa. In *Linguistics in Sub-Saharan Africa,* ed. Jack Berry and Joseph H. Greenberg. Current Trends in Linguistics 7. The Hague: Mouton.

Whitney, William D. 1889. *Sanskrit Grammar.* 2d ed. Cambridge: Harvard University Press.

Winston, F. D. D. 1960. The 'mid-tone' in Efik. *African Language Studies* 1:185–92.

Winter, Werner, ed. 1965. *Evidence for Laryngeals.* The Hague: Mouton.

Wright, Joseph. 1910. *Grammar of the Gothic Language.* Oxford: Clarendon Press.

SYMBOL CHARTS

The Cardinal Vowels 1–8

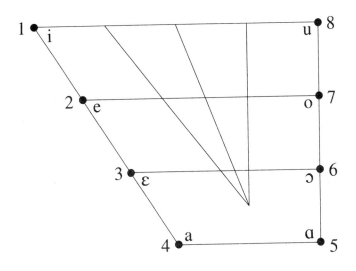

THE EIGHT ORIGINAL PRIMARY CARDINAL VOWELS

Cardinal 1 is defined to be the maximally high and front unrounded vowel articulation which can be produced. Cardinal 5 is defined to be the maximally low and back unrounded vowel articulation which can be produced.

The height of the front of the tongue decreases by even intervals between the cardinals on the line from 1 to 4; the height of the back of the tongue increases by even intervals between the cardinals on the line from 5 to 8. Lip rounding steadily increases from neutral to maximum from 5 to 8.

Acoustically, the first formant steadily increases in frequency from 1 to 4 and decreases from 5 to 8 (i.e. it is inversely correlated with vowel height). The second formant steadily decreases from 1 through 8. See Ladefoged (1982, 174ff).

The Cardinal Vowels 9–16

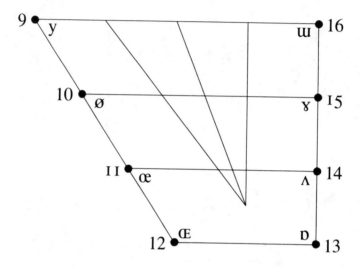

THE EIGHT SECONDARY CARDINAL VOWELS

These vowels have the same articulations as the corresponding primary cardinal vowels, but with reversed lip rounding: [y] is as strongly rounded as possible, and the rounding decreases in even intervals with each vowel along the line from 9 to 13. Cardinals 14 to 16 are unrounded vowels.

IPA Symbols for Unrounded Vowels

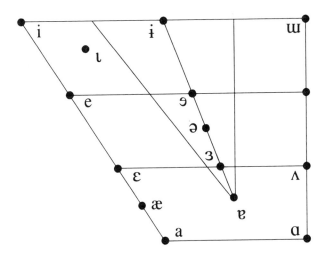

Symbols for unrounded vowels in the IPA tradition. The names of the symbols are:

i	Lower-case *i*	ɨ	Barred *i*	ɯ	Turned *m*
ɩ	Iota	ɘ	Reversed *e*	ɣ	Baby Gamma
e	Lower-case *e*	ə	Schwa	ʌ	Inverted *v*
ɛ	Epsilon	ɜ	Reversed Epsilon	ɑ	Script *a*
æ	Ash	ɐ	Turned *a*		
a	Lower-case *a*				

All but [ɘ] (q.v.) are officially sanctioned by the IPA, which also sanctions [ɪ] for [ɩ].

IPA Symbols for Rounded Vowels

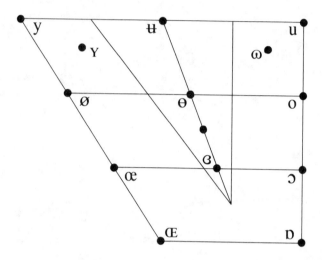

Symbols for rounded vowels in the IPA tradition, after Catford (1977, 179). The unlabeled central dot marks the official IPA position for [ɵ]. The IPA has not officially sanctioned [ʚ], but it is used by several authorities (see entry for details). The names of the symbols are:

y Lower-case *y*	ʉ Barred *u*	u Lower-case *u*
ʏ Small Capital *y*	ɵ Barred *o*	ɷ Closed Omega
ø Slashed *o*	ʚ Closed Reversed	o Lower-case *o*
œ *o-e* Ligature	Epsilon	ɔ Open *o*
Œ Small Capital *o-e*		ɒ Turned Script *a*
Ligature		

The IPA sanctions [ʊ] (upsilon) as a substitute for [ɷ].

Bloch and Trager's Vowel Symbols

	Unrounded	Rounded	Unrounded	Rounded	Unrounded	Rounded
High	i	ü (y)	ɨ	u̇	ï (ɯ)	u
Lower-high	I	Ü	ɪ	U̇	Ï	U
Higher-mid	e	ö (ø)	ė	ȯ	ë (ɣ)	o
Mean-mid	E	Ω̈	Ė (=ə)	Ω̇	Ë	Ω
Lower-mid	ε	ɔ̈ (œ)	ɛ̇	ɔ̇	ɛ̈ (ʌ)	ɔ
Higher-low	æ	ω̈	æ̇	ω̇	æ̈	ω
Low	a	ɒ̈	ȧ	ɒ̇	ä (ɑ)	ɒ

Front	Central	Back

The Bloch and Trager (1942, 22) vowel transcription system is based upon the primary cardinal vowels. The eight primary cardinal vowel symbols are used with their articulatory descriptions, giving four degrees of height (high, higher-mid, lower-mid, and low) and two degrees of backness (front and back). Between each of the four heights an intermediate value is posited, which gives lower-high, higher-low, and their idiosyncratic "mean-mid." Basic symbols are provided for these eight new vowels.

Note that all of the back vowels which have basic symbols are rounded and all of the front vowels with basic symbols are unrounded. Two diacritics are sufficient to extend these 14 basic vowel symbols to give the 42 symbols above. The umlaut is used to indicate reversal of backness, providing symbols for the secondary cardinal vowels, the front rounded vowels and the back unrounded vowels. (The IPA symbols for these are listed as synonyms.) The over-dot diacritic indicates a central vowel. Used with basic symbols for front vowels, it provides symbols for unrounded central vowels; with basic symbols for back vowels, it provides symbols for rounded central vowels.

American Usage Vowel Symbols

		Front		Central		Back	
		Unround	Round	Unround	Round	Unround	Round
High	(Higher)	i	ü	ɨ	ʉ	ï	u
	Lower	I	Ü	ɪ	ʊ	ï	U
Mid	Higher	e	ö	ə		ë	o
	Lower	ɛ	ɔ̈	ʌ			ɔ
Low		æ		a/ɑ			

Lower-Low	a	ɑ	ɒ

This chart is an attempt to generalize the usage of several American authors to represent the points of agreement and disagreement among them and to highlight differences between what we have called "American Usage" and the IPA.

American vowel charts frequently have only five heights; the low front cardinal vowel (4) is considered central. Smalley and Pike distinguish two heights of low vowels, but disagree on the properties of [ɒ]. The independent lower-low rank (Smalley's term) is meant to indicate its optionality. The three symbols in that rank are not always distinguished, but when they are, they are ordered from front to back as indicated. When those symbols are treated as lower-low, inverted *v* may be considered (upper-) low.

The range of inverted *v* and schwa is variable (cf. their entries for details). Open *o* is usually considered a low back rounded vowel, though some authors may agree with the cardinal description of it as lower-mid. Sometimes the distinction between higher- and lower-mid is maintained only in the front vowels, in which case the central and back vowels may simply be described as "mid." (Cf. Gleason 1955.)

Though some of the symbols for the secondary cardinals may be used in American transcription, we have chosen the compositional symbols using the umlaut diacritic to illustrate their denotations.

The Chomsky/Halle Vowel System

		[−back]		[+back]		
		[−round]	[+round]	[−round]	[+round]	
$\begin{bmatrix} +\text{high} \\ -\text{low} \end{bmatrix}$	[+tense]	i	ü	ɨ	u	(*high vowels*)
	[−tense]	I	Ü	ɨ	U	
$\begin{bmatrix} +\text{high} \\ -\text{low} \end{bmatrix}$	[+tense]	e	ö	Λ	o	(*mid vowels*)
	[−tense]	ε				
$\begin{bmatrix} +\text{high} \\ -\text{low} \end{bmatrix}$		æ	œ	a	ɔ	(*low vowels*)

Vowel symbols according to the tradition established by Chomsky and Halle (1968) and later work. Adapted from Halle and Mohanan (1985) with minor changes. (Front rounded symbols from Chomsky and Halle have been included. Halle and Mohanan's [ɨ̵] has been replaced by standard [ɨ].) Where separate symbols for tense and non-tense (i.e. lax) vowels are not shown, a macron (over-bar) is used to indicate a tense vowel. The symbol [ə] is also used in transcription as a totally unstressed vowel of indeterminate feature composition (see entry for Schwa). Note that the distinctions represented reflect phonological rather than phonetic considerations.

IPA Consonant Symbols

Pulmonic Obstruents

Plosives

Plosives	Bilabial	Alveolar	Retroflex	Palatal	Velar	Uvular	Glottal
Voiceless	p	t	ʈ	c	k	q	ʔ
Voiced	b	d	ɖ	ɟ	g	ɢ	

Fricatives

Fricatives	Bilabial	Labio-dental	Inter-dental	Alveolar	Retro-flex	Palato-alveolar	Alveolo-palatal	Palatal	Velar	Uvular	Pharyn-geal	Glottal
Voiceless	ɸ	f	θ	s	ʂ	ʃ	ɕ	ç	x	χ	ħ	h
Voiced	β	v	ð	z	ʐ	ʒ	ʑ	j	ɣ	ʁ	ʕ	ɦ

Doubly Articulated Fricatives

	Voiceless	Voiced
Palatalized Palato-alveolar	ʃ	ʒ
Velar and Palato-alveolar	ɧ	
Labial-Velar	ʍ	

Affricates

Affricates may be written as digraphs, as ligatures, or with 'slur marks' or 'tie-bars'. The three forms are illustrated below for the voiceless palatal-alveolar affricate.

tʃ	ʧ	t͡ʃ

IPA Consonant Symbols

Pulmonic Resonants

Nasals

	Bilabial	Labiodental	Alveolar	Retroflex	Palatal	Velar	Uvular
	m	ɱ	n	ɳ	ɲ	ŋ	ɴ

Laterals

l	Voiced alveolar approximant
ɬ	Voiceless alveolar fricative
ɮ	Voiced alveolar fricative
ɭ	Retroflex approximant
ʎ	Palatal approximant

Median Approximants

ʋ	Labiodental
ɹ	Post-alveolar
ɻ	Retroflex
j	Palatal
ɰ	Velar
ɥ	Labial-palatal
w	Labial-velar

Taps, Flaps, and Trills

r	Alveolar trill
ɽ	Alveolar fricative trill
ɾ	Alveolar tap or flap
ɺ	Alveolar lateral flap
ɽ	Retroflex flap
ʀ	Uvular flap or trill

IPA Consonant Symbols
Non-Pulmonic Consonants

Glottalic Consonants

Implosives

ɓ	Bilabial
ɗ	Alveolar
ɠ	Velar

Ejectives

p'	Bilabial
t'	Alveolar
k'	Velar

Velaric Consonants

Velaric Stops

	⊙	Bilabial
Median Clicks	ǀ	Dental or Alveolar
	C	Postalveolar, Retroflex or Palatal
Lateral Click	ǁ	Alveolar or Postalveolar

American Usage Consonant Symbols

Pulmonic Obstruents

Plosives	Bilabial	Dental	Alveolar	Retroflex	Palatal	Velar	Uvular	Glottal
Voiceless	p	t̪	t	ṭ	ḱ	k	q	ʔ
Voiced	b	d̪	d	ḍ	ǵ	g	ɢ	

Fricatives	Bilabial	Labio-dental	Inter-dental	Dental	Alveolar	Retroflex	Palato-alveolar	Palatal	Velar	Uvular	Pharyngeal	Glottal
Voiceless	ɸ	f	θ	s̪	s	ṣ	š	x̑	x	x̣	ħ	h
Voiced	β	v	ð	z̪	z	ẓ	ž	ɣ̑	ɣ	ɣ̣	ʕ	ɦ

Affricates

	Alveolar	Palato-alveolar	Lateral
Voiceless	¢	č	ƛ
Voiced	dz	ǰ	λ

Affricates may be written as digraphs, but there are special characters which are used for some alveolar and palato-alveolar affricates when they function as single segments phonologically.

American Usage Consonant Symbols

Pulmonic Resonants

Nasals

	Bilabial	Labiodental	Alveolar	Retroflex	Palatal	Velar	Uvular
Nasals	m	ɱ	n	ṇ	ñ	ŋ	ɴ̣

Laterals

l	Voiced alveolar approximant
ɬ	Voiceless alveolar fricative
ḷ	Retroflex approximant

R-Sounds

Very little can be said to be standard in American usage for r-sounds except:

r	Apical
ṛ	Retroflex or Uvular

Glides

w	Labio-velar
y	Palatal

Non-Pulmonic Consonants

Implosives
(Glottalic Ingressive)

ɓ	Bilabial
ɗ	Alveolar
ɠ	Velar

Ejectives
(Glottalic Egressive)

p'	Bilabial
t'	Alveolar
k'	Velar